D0860448

.

CASE STUDIES IN
CULTURAL ANTHROPOLOGY

GENERAL EDITORS
George and Louise Spindler
STANFORD UNIVERSITY

_____

KIPPEL: A CHANGING
VILLAGE IN THE ALPS

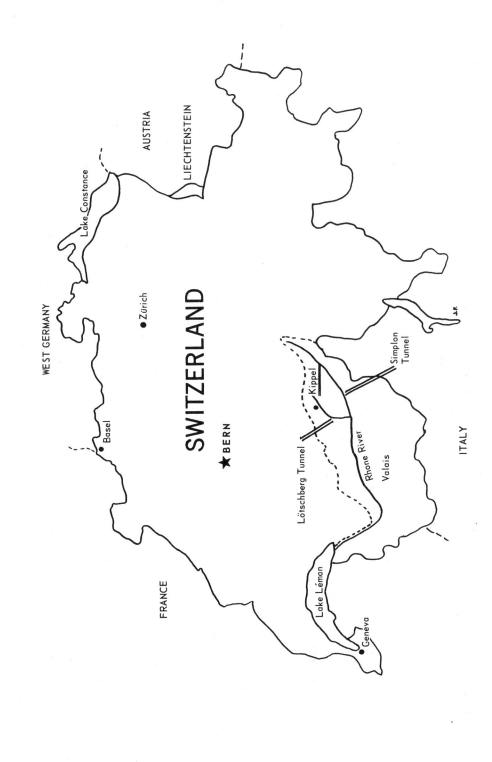

WEST GERMANY

AUSTRIA

LIECHTENSTEIN

Lake Constance

• Zürich

SWITZERLAND

★ BERN

• Basel

FRANCE

Loïschberg Tunnel

• Kippel

Simplon Tunnel

Rhone River

Valais

ITALY

Lake Léman

• Geneva

KIPPEL: A CHANGING VILLAGE IN THE ALPS

By

JOHN FRIEDL
The Ohio State University

HOLT, RINEHART AND WINSTON, INC.

NEW YORK   CHICAGO   SAN FRANCISCO   ATLANTA

DALLAS   MONTREAL   TORONTO   LONDON   SYDNEY

WILLIAM MADISON RANDALL LIBRARY UNC AT WILMINGTON

Library of Congress Cataloging in Publication Data

Friedl, John.
  Kippel: a changing village in the Alps.

  (Case studies in cultural anthropology)
  Bibliography: p. 128
  1. Kippel, Switzerland. I. Title. II. Series.
DQ851.K44F74   301.29'494'7   73–8631

ISBN: 0–03–008206–4

Copyright © 1974 by Holt, Rinehart and Winston, Inc.
All rights reserved
Printed in the United States of America

4 5 6 7   059   9 8 7 6 5 4 3 2 1

DQ851
.K44
.F74

Foreword

ABOUT THE SERIES

These case studies in cultural anthropology are designed to bring to students, in beginning and intermediate courses in the social sciences, insights into the richness and complexity of human life as it is lived in different ways and in different places. They are written by men and women who have lived in the societies they write about and who are professionally trained as observers and interpreters of human behavior. The authors are also teachers, and in writing their books they have kept the students who will read them foremost in their minds. It is our belief that when an understanding of ways of life very different from one's own is gained, abstractions and generalizations about social structure, cultural values, subsistence techniques, and the other universal categories of human social behavior become meaningful.

ABOUT THE AUTHOR

John Friedl is assistant professor of anthropology at The Ohio State University in Columbus, Ohio. He received his Ph.D. in anthropology from the University of California at Berkeley, where he taught briefly before coming to Ohio State. The field work in Switzerland, upon which this book is based, was carried out in 1969–1970, and has resulted in several articles in professional journals as well. Dr. Friedl has also studied a rural cattle ranching community in central California (1968), and more recently he has returned to Switzerland to study problems of education and mass media in the process of modernization (1972). Aside from an interest in European ethnology, he also specializes in comparative peasant societies and in urban anthropology. Dr. Friedl founded and is editor of the journal *Studies in European Society*, and is co-editor of *City Ways: A Reader in Urban Anthropology*.

ABOUT THE BOOK

Kippel, a village in canton Valais, Switzerland, is, like every other alpine village, different from other villages in other valleys and distinctive in its way of life from other parts of Europe. As John Friedl points out, the economic, social, and political institutions have a flavor all their own, conditioned by the ecology of the alpine valleys in which settlements are located. This case study acknowledges this difference and gives the reader an understanding of some of the important traditional institutions that most clearly reflect this ecological relationship.

Kippel is, however, like most other villages in Europe in the sense that it has undergone radical change in the last thirty years. There are people in the village who have suffered from the sharp departure from tradition brought about by the postwar industrialization and others who have benefited. The case study takes into account forces for the maintenance of tradition and other forces working for its obliteration. It deals, too, with the way the people feel about these processes. The author shows how agriculture today is mainly a symbolic activity that brings security both because it contributes to subsistence and because of its traditional meaning for the older members of the community. He shows how change in the village has been due primarily to a shift in the economy from agriculture to industry and tourism, from traditional subsistence to a cash economy. Agriculture has tended to remain relatively backward, both because of its symbolic value and because of limiting ecological factors. The village is therefore a place of sharp contrasts between the traditional and the modern. These contrasts are expanded in the case study with attention to traditional agro-pastoralism, industrialization after World War II, and modernization since 1960.

This case study on Kippel, in its alpine environment, when compared with Burgbach, lying in a much broader valley in southern Germany, and Orašac, a Serbian village not far from Belgrade, will demonstrate to the student the remarkable cultural diversity of Europe and also the extent to which postwar urbanization and industrialization have produced markedly similar results in these different communities.*

GEORGE AND LOUISE SPINDLER
General Editors

Phlox, Wisconsin

* George Spindler, *Burgbach: Urbanization and Identity in a German Village*, Holt, Rinehart and Winston, 1973; and Joel Halpern and Barbara Halpern, *A Serbian Village in Historical Perspective*, Holt, Rinehart and Winston, 1972. Both are Case Studies in Cultural Anthropology.

Preface

The fieldwork for this study was carried out in Kippel, canton Valais, Switzerland, from September 1969 through September 1970. The preparation, research, and completion of the work was made possible by a grant from the National Institutes of Health, Training Grant GM–1224.

I have chosen to use the name of Kippel rather than a pseudonym, for it is my belief that it would be futile to disguise the village. More important, it was clear that the villagers were pleased to have a book written about themselves. However, I have avoided using personal names within the text. Of course, the villagers will know whom I am talking about much of the time, but I have attempted to protect them from any form of criticism from the outside by simply omitting personal references.

It is difficult to list all those people to whom I am indebted for their assistance in the research for this work. Professor Gerald Berhoud has been most helpful, both in Berkeley in the preparatory stages of my project and in Kippel during the summer of 1970. Professors May Diaz, Richard Roehl, and especially Jack Potter, all of Berkeley, have read my work and contributed valuable comments and suggestions.

In Switzerland, Professor Arnold Niederer of the University of Zürich contributed much of his time and effort to helping me along the way while I was in Kippel. As executor of the estate of the late Albert Nyfeler, he has graciously granted me permission to use several of the photographs in this book. His willingness to assist me with all problems, big and little, and his warm and unselfish interest in my work, have earned for him my deepest respect.

Above all, I am grateful to the entire village of Kippel for the kindness and understanding with which they took me into their homes and their lives. I know how difficult it must have been for them to understand my presence, but for the most part this did not deter them from making my stay a most pleasant experience. I regret that in order to preserve their anonymity I cannot name those individuals who were especially helpful to me, and I hope that through this book I might be able to express my gratitude to them.

JOHN FRIEDL

Columbus, Ohio
September 1973

Contents

This land, do you recognize it still? The old woman at her spinning wheel, the goatherd blowing his horn, the miracle doctor who heals with herb tea and faith, and the long silence of time that sways the unruly water of the river. Museum pieces! The masters of space and energy have arrived. They have paved the way. The wheel of the truck obliterates the footprints of the mule in the dust. In place of stalls and barns they build garages and workshops. The electric lamp and neon sign replace the old gas lantern and banish the startled ghosts. A new epoch begins, full of movement and life. They were living in the past—we unlock the future.

Maurice Zermatten

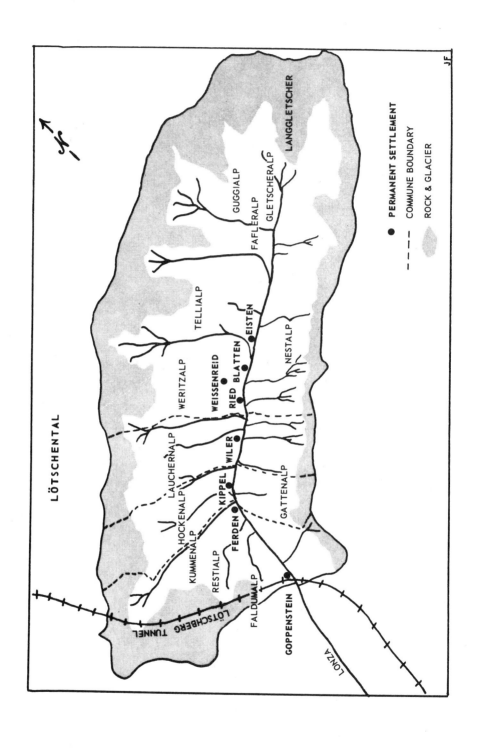

LÖTSCHENTAL

LANGGLETSCHER

GLETSCHERALP
FAFLERALP
GUGGIALP

TELLIALP

WERITZALP

EISTEN

NESTALP

WEISSENRIED
RIED BLATTEN

LAUCHERNALP

WILER

GATTENALP

HOCKENALP
KIPPEL

KUMMENALP
FERDEN

RESTIALP

FALDUMALP

LÖTSCHBERG TUNNEL

GOPPENSTEIN

LONZA

● PERMANENT SETTLEMENT
--- COMMUNE BOUNDARY
ROCK & GLACIER

JF

1 / Introduction

This book is about a village and the changes it has undergone in the last thirty years. But more than that, it is about the people who live there, those who have suffered and benefited from the radical departure from tradition brought about by the postwar industrialization of their country. They have been swept along in the new way of life that has engulfed a generation of mountain dwellers, and in many cases they have reacted with bewildered resignation as they watched their historical roots being pulled up from under them.

This book is also about the changes that have *not* taken place and the fight to hang on to what little is left. However, it is not under any circumstances an impassioned plea for the maintenance of tradition in the face of modernization, any more than it is an advertisement for the blessings of the new industrial society. Both points of view can be supported, but how do you measure the value of tradition against the high standard of living attained in recent decades? Is today's system of mass communication and international awareness to be preferred over yesterday's isolation and close-knit village life? I leave this problem to the reader, with the admonition that whatever side one chooses, one must at least try to achieve the perspective of the other.

It might help to point out just how the villagers feel about what has happened to them since the second world war. As we would expect, the youngsters who are beginning to participate in the new economy to the fullest are all for it. They criticize their elders for being old-fashioned and conservative, much the same as in our own country. The generation gap is not restricted to the United States, or even to urban society, but is found everywhere.

Surprisingly, however, we find that even the older people in the village—the farmers who stayed on the land rather than move into industrial jobs, the women who cried when their sons went off to work in the city—feel better off today than a generation ago. There is talk about the good old days, but not without praise for the modern inventions that they didn't have then. And, too, there is contempt for the nativists—the tourists who spend a week's vacation hiking around the mountain pastures or skiing down the steep slopes, all the while complaining about the disappearance of the old rustic atmosphere, the pollution creeping out from their cities to their country retreats, and the replacement of peasant costumes with business suits. An old villager recalled with a chuckle one day how he had pointed out all the changes to one such tourist. As he ran his

1

eyes over the landscape he noted the disappearance of the rye fields, the modern dress on village women, the paved road with its automobiles, almost bringing a tear to the eye of the man from the city. "But what did he know?" he suddenly blurted out. "He didn't have to live here when we were hungry, when we had no running water, no indoor toilets, no modern conveniences and not even enough money to buy them if they were available. He just goes back to his comfortable home in the city and complains about it!"

Originally I had not intended to study social change in a Swiss village, but rather I was prepared to work almost exclusively on the topic of alpine ecology. In the preliminary stage of my investigation, I found the literature available in the US on Swiss rural life deplorably inadequate. The choice of a suitable location for my study was a difficult one to make, precisely because of the lack of information. It was impossible to know enough about the current situation in the changing rural scene to form a clear-cut orientation toward a specific problem, and although I made an attempt to do so, I found that my original plans had to be readjusted considerably to meet the demands of the situation. Inferences from census material helped define general trends, but the final choice of a village was made by chance.

When I first arrived in the village of Kippel I was struck by its primitive appearance. The typical American's stereotype of Switzerland as a modern, efficient country was contradicted by the village with its ancient wooden buildings, and by the people still carrying hay and potatoes on their backs. I suppose I was no more surprised than a European would be if he encountered some of the backwoods areas in the Appalachians or the Ozarks. The villagers were used to tourists, so they were not unduly shocked by my presence at first—that is, until I made my first innocent blunder. I had just made arrangements to rent a flat in a private home, had parked the car, and was carrying my baggage into the house.

"How long will you be staying?" asked the lady in whose house I was going to live.

"A year," was my straightforward reply, upon which she fell into uncontrollable fits of laughter. Her sister, who had been standing with her on the porch, scurried off to spread the latest piece of gossip, and from then on I was the conversation piece of the village throughout my entire stay. I often wonder what they would have talked about that year if I had not come along.

Despite the fact that I was such a lively topic of conversation among the villagers, my popularity did not extend to interaction with the people. I constantly had to combat suspicion, usually in the form of rumors that spread like wildfire through the village. (At one point it was even suggested that I was a spy hired by another village. Why else would I be in Kippel when clearly I could get my Ph.D. much faster elsewhere?) In a few cases there was lingering distrust or even outright hostility. Many an anthropologist has noted the tendency of the people he has studied to be slow to warm up and, particularly among mountain people in close-knit communities where only the most rugged breed of men can survive, it is not to be expected that an entire village will open up its arms to a stranger. A Swiss–German physician from another canton described the problems he encountered in gathering data in the same valley for a medical study of his own, with which I must concur:

> The rural and especially the mountain people do not take well to questionnaires or formal interviews. First there must be trust, and then one must merely wait until the proper time when the heart opens up and the tongue is loosened. This moment cannot be rushed, but it always comes, if only after many years (Müller 1969:37).

Once settled in Kippel I set about the immediate task of getting to know as many people as possible, attempting to inform them of my intent, and to explain my proposed research. At the same time, I tried to discern just how feasible an ecological study would be, and the more I learned about the life of the village, the less practicable it appeared. Only after many months of readjusting my goals to fit the particular situation of my village did I finally arrive at the present form of analysis. It was not possible to study traditional agro-pastoral practices when only one or two farmers remained in the entire village, nor did it seem wise to lay undue emphasis upon the traditional, ignoring the obvious changes that had occurred through industrialization in recent decades. Instead, I found that by resorting to a rather extensive body of literature that dealt with the more traditional times in the valley's history, I could reconstruct quite accurately the patterns of village life as they existed prior to the major intrusion of industrialization. My work in the village, then, could be directed more profitably toward a study of contemporary life styles, comparing and contrasting them to earlier forms. I was able to establish a turning point at about the time of the second world war, which meant that I had access to informants who had seen the village pass through the period of industrialization I wanted to describe.

It was most fortunate that so recent a date could be set as the pivotal time in the history of the valley, for it is an era well within the memory of many villagers. The eager assistance of a number of older residents of Kippel proved to be invaluable, not only in evaluating observations of the present, but in evaluating sources of the past. Crucial questions could be answered by enough informants to guarantee accuracy, and the pitfalls of working with a single informant— the last of a dying legend—were avoided.

2 / The village and its background

Life in a traditional mountain village in the Swiss Alps differs in many ways from that in any other region of Europe. The economic, social, and political institutions have a flavor all their own, conditioned in most respects by, and doubtless directly related to, the ecology of the alpine valleys in which settlements are located. Development within each valley is independent. Often, two adjacent subsidiary valleys will differ greatly in their economic emphasis, not as a result of the economic division of labor relative to the main valley population or that of the cities, but due instead to a climatic and ecological difference between the two. While influences of modernization in the form of mechanization and industry have spread from the cities to the plains and even into the lower mountain valleys, the high subsidiary valleys have retained much of their traditional character.

In a region made up of such naturally defined subdivisions as the lateral subsidiary valleys descending to the river of the main alpine valley, the socially defined community tends to be the exclusive occupant of its own lateral valley. The community is closed and corporate,* owing to the problems it faces on a separate local level. This is true in practice as well as in theory, as seen in the incentives for village and valley endogamy (in-marriage) and regulations prohibiting the sale of land to outsiders.

Such is the case in the canton of Valais, Switzerland. Situated in the southwest portion of the country, it embraces the watershed of the Rhone River from its source high in the Alps down to the eastern shore of Lake Geneva. More than a dozen major lateral valleys branch off from the main Rhone Valley, carving out habitable niches in this otherwise barren and mountainous region. The relative isolation of the subsidiary valley settlements has led to the paradox of a backward, rural, agricultural population living in what must be considered one of the most modern countries of the world.

The Lötschental (pronounced LURCH-en-tahl) is one such subsidiary valley,

---

* Wolf defines a closed corporate community as a basically egalitarian coalition which tends to restrict membership to people born and raised within its confines. It is characterized by a high rate of endogamy, by the ultimate domain to the land resting with the community rather than with the individual, by leveling devices or redistribution of surplus through communal ceremonials, and by a high degree of internal order and stability (1966:85–86).

located in the German-speaking area of the canton, known as Upper Valais. It runs parallel and to the north of the Rhone Valley, separated by a chain of mountains interrupted only by a steep, narrow gorge leading into the valley. The inhabitants speak a Swiss–German dialect and are almost exclusively Roman Catholic.

HISTORICAL SETTING

The Lötschental was probably first entered by neolithic hunters. The first known inhabitants date back to between the seventh and tenth centuries B.C., as borne out by several graves and other archaeological finds. Subsequent settlements were inhabited by the Celts, Celto-Romans, Alemanni, and Burgundians, with the Alemanni accounting for about four-fifths of the ancestry of the present population (Siegen 1965). The Burgundians never really had much influence upon the Lötschental during their overall control of Valais after the fifth century A.D. Despite its proximity to the Rhone Valley, the Lötschental was so inaccessible from the south that the main source of contact was through traffic over the Lötschen Pass to the north.

As transalpine transportation increased during the Middle Ages, the Lötschental took on importance, so much so that in 1233 the Baron of Thurm, into whose possession the Lötschental and much of Upper Valais fell, made a separate parish out of the valley. Political control over the Lötschental changed several times until, in 1790, the inhabitants purchased their freedom from the surrounding districts to which they had been subservient. Ironically, only a short time after the Revolution, the French swept into Valais and the valley would have been set free anyway.

The Lötschen Pass declined as a trade route after the seventeenth century and did not regain its former stature as a transalpine route until the beginning of this century, when a railroad tunnel was constructed at the mouth of the valley. The BLS (Bern-Lötschberg-Simplon) rail line connects the Simplon route to the Bernese Highland and points north, and thereby overcomes the total isolation of the Lötschental.

Throughout the nineteenth century Valais remained an agrarian canton, with little production for the market and little reliance on a money economy—much in contrast to the rest of Switzerland, which had already begun to practice modern methods of production. Industrialization did not begin in Valais until 1850, dependent as it was upon the railroads. Not until 1878 was there a railroad line running the length of the canton. Around the turn of the century the growth of industry picked up. The lack of coal and other natural resources in Switzerland led to a demand for water power for electricity, and the technological limits on transferring this power meant that factories requiring much energy had to be constructed where the power was located. Valais, with its many mountain streams, was ideally suited in this respect (Kaufmann 1965:38).

During the first world war, trade limitations placed all resources at a premium, so that a coal mine in the Lötschental, too poor to justify operation under normal circumstances, was put into full swing, providing income for many households in the valley. The economic prosperity was short-lived, however, for the mine was closed after the war. The period between the wars was one of industrial stagnation, with an actual increase in agricultural production.

At the outbreak of hostilities in 1939 the Lötschental, isolated as it still was from the mainstream of industrial activity in Valais, was much the same as it had been for centuries, both economically and socially. The railroad had opened up a channel of communication, but the full effect of contact with the outside world had not yet set in. Emigration had not shown any noticeable increase, and the standard of living was no higher than a century before—in fact, in many respects it was lower. A few modern conveniences had been brought in, the most important being electricity, but for the most part life went on as it always had.

The only major influence of the outside world upon the Lötschental at that time was the Depression, which had managed to filter into the valley. Its important effect was to shut off the escape valve of emigration by limiting the employment opportunities outside the valley. Thus the Lötschental was forced to absorb the excess of its growing population, and the result was catastrophic. With an increase in population of 37.6 percent from 1900 to 1941, the demographic pressure upon the limited geographic area forced the development of new economic relationships. The traditional balance could not be maintained, which ultimately led to a serious drop in the standard of living. Although the Lötschental had always been relatively poor in the sense of material wealth, its inhabitants had never before reached the subsistence level of agriculture, where they could barely survive on what they produced. Church records dating back centuries have not described a period as severe as the decade before the second world war.

The end of World War II saw a rejuvenation of Valaisan industrial development. Minor losses of industry occurred due to the technological advances allowing factories to transfer electrical power from its source to a more suitable site. But these losses were more than offset by new industry in the canton, particularly in the Rhone Valley. Major construction projects for hydroelectric plants and other factories created new jobs for the former Valaisan agriculturalists.

It was the major economic change of the postwar era that brought about the transformation of the Lötschental from a self-sufficient agro-pastoral valley to an industrial area, the seat of a rural proletariat dependent for its livelihood upon urban and semiurban industrial centers. Men began to work in factories, at first maintaining a small agricultural operation on the side, and later giving that up too. Today skilled labor is replacing unskilled labor, services are becoming more important to the local economy, and communication is rapidly increasing—in short, the Lötschental is modernizing.

Accompanying this modernization process is a breakdown in certain aspects of the old order, a replacement of techniques and values. At the same time many things have been retained either completely or in part, and because of the relative newness of change they are still very recognizable. Frequently, old practices have been given new meanings or interpretations; many have declined or disappeared altogether. The introduction of a money economy has required that work previously done on a communal basis now be reevaluated according to a wage scale. The flow of men from agriculture to industry has demanded a new approach to the age-old methods of combatting the elements. The ecological situation, which had been so very important in binding the villagers together into a communal labor force, has become of secondary importance. Changes primarily in the occupational structure of the village and valley have rendered impossible much of the work previously requiring the entire male population of each village, and this in turn has led to a new set of values toward community and individual.

The problem to be considered here in this case study is that of the uneven rate of change in different spheres of village life. Change in the village has been due primarily to a shift in the economy from agriculture to industry, bringing with it a heavy reliance upon cash rather than the traditional subsistence orientation. It was only with the postwar prosperity that this shift could be made, for prior to 1945 the poverty of the surrounding area literally forced people to remain in agriculture to make a living. Changes in the village economy appear to have occurred more rapidly than in other aspects of the social life; religious and political activities have changed less rapidly and tend to reflect greater conservatism. Agriculture in the village has remained relatively backward and, rather than apply modern ideas to turn it into a productive occupation under today's market conditions, the villagers have left agriculture for jobs in industry. Furthermore, agricultural conservatism is to a great extent determined by the limiting ecological factors present in this and other alpine valleys. Finally, a tendency to hang onto the past through agriculture (and thereby the old values and traditions) exists as a force counteractive to the rapidly changing village life, and this tendency proves to be an inefficient luxury rather than a rational economic activity. Agriculture today is a symbolic activity directly related to subsistence and the security it brings to the older members of the village. It is practiced by each household independently and does not relate to a wider market. In this sense it can coexist with a rapidly changing economic order. However, agriculture is now disappearing and will continue to do so at an accelerated rate, as industry and tourism take over the economy of the village, establishing new values for time and labor.

With this general orientation of the study we can now turn to the setting, the Lötschental.

ECOLOGICAL SETTING

The Lötschental is a lateral valley subsidiary to the Rhone River, the main corridor through the heart of the canton of Valais in southern Switzerland. It follows the course of the Lonza, a stream originating at the back of the valley and flowing southwest for seven miles before turning due south, where it ultimately empties into the Rhone at the twin villages of Gampel and Steg, midway between the canton capital of Sion and the Swiss end of the Simplon Tunnel at Brig. The lower part of the valley is steep and narrow, uninhabitable and too rocky even for pasturage. Except for its influence in isolating the Lötschental from the neighboring Rhone Valley, the lower gorge is of no significance to the rest of the valley, and reference to the Lötschental does not include this section.

View of the Lötschental from the southwest.

The upper valley covers approximately 57 square miles, of which over half is unproductive rock and glacier. Its floor ranges from an altitude of 3950 feet at Goppenstein, the train station at the mouth of the Lötschberg Tunnel, to 6400 feet at the foot of the glacier known as the *Langgletscher*. The valley floor extends for 11 miles, and at its broadest point is about a quarter of a mile wide. It is bisected by the Lonza, which begins at the *Langgletscher*, joined at right angles by dozens of smaller streams cutting deep ridges into the slopes of either side throughout their entire length, carrying water down from the ring of glaciers around the top of the valley as well as from numerous springs on the alpine pastures.

Both slopes rise sharply from the valley floor, but differ greatly from each other in most respects. The southern, shady side is the steeper of the two. Because of its unfavorable orientation it is covered with forest and only near the valley floor can it support any substantial growth of grass. The northern, sunny side is interspersed with grass and scattered trees and bushes, but has several large patches of forest as well. The timber line on the shady side is about 7200 feet, slightly higher than on the sunny side.

Above the forest on both sides lie terraces carved out by the glaciation of the Riss period. On the shady side those that can be used at all tend to serve primarily as sheep pastures, while on the opposite side they are dotted with summer settlements where cattle are kept and grazed. Finally, above this ridge along the entire perimeter of the valley there are steep, jagged, rocky mountain peaks, either bare or covered by glacier. Few passes traverse this ring of mountain and glacier, and only one, the Lötschen Pass, was ever of any economic importance. Located at the northwest corner of the valley at 8750 feet, it leads from the Lötschental to Kandersteg and the Bernese Highland, and was until the eighteenth century a major transalpine route. It remained important for local residents until the construction of the railway in 1913.

The Lötschental consists of four communes, or *Gemeinden*, the smallest unit in the Swiss political system (see map p. xi). Ferden, Kippel, and Wiler each contain only one village, while Blatten includes the village of Blatten and the hamlets of Ried, Weissenried, and Eisten, and in this respect is more typical of mountain communities in Valais. All four villages of the Lötschental are located on the valley floor just above the north bank of the Lonza. In addition, the hamlets of Ried and Eisten are similarly situated, while Weissenried, the lone exception, lies on the sunny slope about 650 feet above Ried. The villages can be safely situated near the river, since except for the uppermost portion of the valley, the floor is not flat and therefore there is no danger of flooding (Unstead 1932:311). Being located near the valley floor is not typical of most mountain villages in Valais, and this has important implications for land use, which will be discussed below.

Whereas flooding plays no role in the site of the villages, avalanches are the single most important factor in the strategic location of settlements. Over two dozen brooks cut into the slopes of the valley, and each can act as a channel for an avalanche. Some avalanches come down regularly each year, while others occur only once in a generation or two when conditions are particularly bad. However, the fact that each has a name, which is generally associated with the stream whose path it follows, is indicative of their importance. The location of a settlement is thus dependent upon the absence of such an avalanche channel. When viewed from above, these streams create a scalloped effect in the sides of the valley, with villages located at the convex point, between two streams. But there is a further limiting factor, which is the need for something to hold back the snow. Streams cannot do this because there can be no trees in their path. But even between streams this is only possible if there is a patch of forest large enough to serve as a protective barrier. Furthermore, if the settlement is on the valley floor, both slopes must be taken into consideration. It is for this reason that buildings are not scattered along the roadside throughout the valley, but are huddled together in places safe from avalanche.

Climatically, the Lötschental is favored in many ways over the rest of Valais. It is the only subsidiary valley that has the same east–west orientation as the

Rhone, affecting above all the amount of sunshine it receives. This means that the northern slope of the valley is exposed to the sun longer than either slope of a north–south oriented valley. On the other hand, the southern shady side will go for days on end during the winter without direct sunshine. Consequently, the economic importance of one slope over another is intensified in the Lötschental as compared to other lateral valleys in Valais.

Another beneficial aspect of the Lötschental climate is the amount of precipitation it receives. Valais is the driest canton in Switzerland, and the Rhone Valley contains the driest region in Valais. But the Lötschental does not follow the example of the similarly oriented Rhone in this case, for the average annual precipitation here exceeds that of the canton as a whole, with a total of almost 37 inches (Loup 1965:54).

Yet not everything about the Lötschental works to its relative advantage, for in terms of altitude it is less fortunate than its neighbors. The average altitude of the valley floor is about 5200 feet; the west wall rises 3250 feet above this, the north wall about 5550 feet and the south wall 6500 feet above it. Some implications of the relatively high overall altitude of the Lötschental concerning land use and village location will be discussed later on, but it is certainly evident that high altitude hampers agriculture, shortens growing seasons, causes lower temperatures, and limits the amount of usable land. Good cultivation is usually impossible above 5000 feet, and more than three-quarters of the Lötschental lies above this level.

We must bear in mind that all of these factors are relative, and no matter whether they may seem advantageous compared to neighboring valleys or not, the setting is in absolute terms very harsh. As Loup so succinctly describes the situation:

> The study of the physical conditions points out the considerable difficulties in the exploitation of the soil: the high average altitude, the massivity, the slope, . . . the great amount of unusable land, the rough climate, more continental than in the French Alps of the north, the dryness—all are obstacles to an active agro-pastoral life (1965:95).

THE VILLAGE

Kippel, at 4500 feet, is the second of the four communes in the Lötschental, located above Ferden and below Wiler and Blatten. It is bounded on the northeast by two streams, the Gafenbach and the Bättla, and on the southwest by the Ferdenbach and an irregular line from the confluence of the Ferdenbach and the Lonza south to the Schräjendbach, then east along the latter stream. (see map) The northwest and southeast boundaries are the watershed lines of the surrounding mountains. The village of Kippel is located on the north bank just above the Lonza between the Gafenbach and the Golmbach. It is shielded above on the sunny side by a patch of forest known as Riedholz, and on the shady side by the Kipplerwald.

The village itself is huddled together between these two streams, relatively secure from any danger of avalanche. In the center of the village are the oldest houses, many of which date back to the sixteenth century. Often supported by a stone foundation, these older buildings are made of larch wood, a deciduous pine that grows in the forests of the Lötschental. It has the advantage for construction of sealing with age; it is also known for its change of color from a golden brown to almost black as it is worn by wind and weather, so that older houses can be recognized by their color as well as the style of construction.

Houses of the fifteenth and sixteenth centuries were generally one-family dwellings with one or two stories and a stone walled cellar. From the seventeenth century on, two- and even three- and four-family houses were built, each several stories high with one flat to a story. Several examples of this larger house-type stand in Kippel, including the most famous (although by no means the largest), the *Murmannhaus*, built in 1777 and known for its master craftsmanship and ornate carving, both inside and out. This tradition of carving on the beams inside the house and on the walls outside is an old custom probably brought into the Lötschental during the fifteenth century from the Bernese Highland. Aside from decorative designs and patterns, inscriptions, usually dealing with religious subjects, are universally present on older buildings along with the date of construction carved below the peak of the roof. Some of the older inscriptions are carved

Kippel. The vacation chalet at the upper left was destroyed by avalanche in 1970.

in Gothic script, the newer ones generally in the ornate German script used until recently by Germanic peoples of Europe. Examples of these inscriptions illustrate the messages they convey:

> Gemeinde Lieb und Aufrichtigkeit
> Haben mich allhier aus garbeit.
> Fart fordt, liebt Got in Einigkeit,
> So bauwt ihr ein Haus der Ewigkeit.

> Mutual love and honesty
> Have built me here with industry.
> Continue, love God in unity,
> So you will build a house in eternity.

The *Grosse Huis* (large house) in Kippel, built in 1665, displays a familiar philosophy:

> Ich leb, weis nit wie lang,
> Sterben muss ich, und weis nit wan,
> Ich fahr, und weis wohin,
> Wen ich der Tugend fleissig bin.

> I know not how long I shall live,
> I must die, and I know not when,
> But I know where I will be going
> If I remain faithful to my duty.*

The old communal hall in Kippel was inscribed with the following:

> Wer buwt ein Haus
> Mus bald daraus
> Old dan er buw
> Ein ewigs Hus.
> Lug, das dir berits
> Ein Haus in Ewigkeit.
> Ein Haus der Einigkeit
> Bewohnt die H. Dreifaltigkeit.

* This particular theme is apparently widespread throughout German-speaking Europe. A similar poem is reportedly carved on the wall of a German house in Hessen:

> Ich komm, weiss nicht, woher,
> Ich bin, ich weiss nicht, wer,
> Ich leb, weiss nicht, wie lang,
> Ich sterb und weiss nicht, wann,
> Ich fahr, weiss nicht, wohin;
> Mich wundert's, daß ich fröhlich bin.
> (Kurtz and Politzer 1958:91)

> I don't know where I come from,
> I don't know who I am,
> I don't know how long I'll live,
> I don't know when I'll die,
> I don't know where I'm going,
> It's a wonder that I'm joyful.

> He who builds a house
> Must quit it soon,
> Unless he builds
> An eternal house.
> See that you prepare for yourself
> A house for eternity.
> In a house of unity
> Dwells the Holy Trinity.

Inscriptions on the inside of houses usually include the names of the original owners of the house or apartment carved on the main beam across the ceiling of the living room. Short sayings were also popular, however, in strategic places. In one house over the bed was carved:

> Ich geh' ins Bett,
> Vielleicht in Tod.

> I go to bed,
> Perhaps to death.

Turning to the construction and shape of the house, the outside walls consist of beams placed atop one another. They are generally 5 to 6 inches thick and as

Inscription on a hut: "The high paths are dangerous, because they are steep and precipitous. Put your fate in God's hand, the angels of God will protect you."

broad as the particular tree allows. Eight to ten inches from the end each beam is notched so that it can be crossed at the corners. The boards are then hollowed out slightly at the top and filled with moss for better insulation.

Whether it be a single family house or a part of a larger one, each unit usually contains part of the cellar plus a kitchen and two combination living/ bedrooms. These latter rooms must suffice for sleeping quarters for the entire family; they serve as workrooms during the day for the women. In one-family houses the rooms are sometimes divided among two stories, while in multiple dwellings each family has a separate floor, rather than a side-by-side arrangement.

The cellar is not dug into the ground, but rather the stone walls are built on the surface with the wooden stories above. The walls are dotted with numerous windows, increasing in size with more recently built houses. The door is located on the side of the house, above ground level. Usually a stairway leads up to a balcony from which the door will lead to the kitchen or a hallway, and if there are two or more stories, it will continue to the top.

The oldest known house in the valley was the so-called *Hennuhuis*, built in Eisten (Commune of Blatten) in 1404, and destroyed by avalanche in 1951. It was 13 feet wide, 21 feet high, and about 21 feet long. Its cellar was made of wood rather than stone and in fact was more like a stall. Only the corners and part of the back wall were stone, and these were merely stacked up, not sealed with mortar. The front wall had two small windows in each of the stories, the upper ones more like irregular shaped holes. The rear of the house stood higher than the front, being built into a slope. Inside, the house was tiny, with small rooms, low doors, and ceilings. In general it differed from later houses only in that it was built over a stall rather than a stone-walled cellar.

Electricity was first introduced into the valley in 1914, and all houses built after that date made use of it. Older houses were gradually converted, so that by the second world war all houses had power. Plumbing came later—the first house with running water was built in 1906, but that was only in the kitchen. Most houses did not have this convenience until the introduction of a water system in 1945, when all but three households took advantage of it immediately. Likewise, toilets were not widespread until the second world war.

The village is divided into neighborhoods, each named according to some special feature with which it is identified, and it is these neighborhood names which are used by residents in describing the location of any particular place or person. Examples are *Am Platz*, meaning "at the village square," and *Finsterhof*, or dark courtyard, so named because of an overhanging porch that creates a dark area along the path into the village. These neighborhoods tend to be very closely defined, and even though not all villagers agree on their exact boundaries, every location in the village falls within a neighborhood.

Numerous other nonagricultural buildings are to be found in Kippel, the most important and certainly the most prominent being the church. St. Martin's Church was first built in 1535, enlarged in 1556, 1740, and again in 1915. It is a tall, white, stone edifice located at the eastern edge of the central cluster of houses. The church is ringed by a low-walled cemetery containing the graves of all dead parishioners, including Blatteners until 1899, and those from Ferden and Wiler until 1956, when they each established a separate parish in their own commune. Each grave is marked by several crosses, due to the overcrowding which has necessitated reuse of the site numerous times. At the rear corner of the church a belfry extends upward, from which the call to the villagers goes out for all religious occasions and many important secular events as well. Behind the church stands a small charnel house, a chapel where exhumed skulls were once stored. Next to that is the *Kaplaneihaus*, the former residence of the chaplain, or priest's assistant.

The village also has a communal hall and a schoolhouse, both of which have been replaced by newer buildings since the war. The post office is the lower story of the postman's home, the bakery beneath the baker's residence. There are four general stores, two of which predate the war. Other important nonagricultural features of the village are the sawmill located on the Lonza just below the village, the old oven, no longer used but formerly the source of bread for the entire village, and the two fountains in the center of the village, which until at least 1945 were the main source of water for the home, for washing clothes, and for all household and agricultural necessities.

Finally, there is a hotel, a *Pension*, and a *Gasthaus*. The Hotel Lötschberg, built in 1906, has approximately 50 beds, and is open during the summer only (it has no heat). It includes a large restaurant and a smaller separate dining room. Gasthaus Kippel, erected in 1910, had about 10 small rooms and a restaurant/

The cemetery in the church courtyard.

Some women still use the fountain for washing tools and work clothes.

bar (it was torn down and rebuilt in 1971). The Pension Bietschhorn, dating from 1928, is about the same size as the *Gasthaus*, although it does have an additional large meeting room. There is also a fourth drinking spot, located in the *Grosse Huis* in the center of the village; however, it offers neither food nor a place to sleep. With the exception of the latter, these buildings are located on the road running through the village, which means they are slightly above and to the west of the central cluster.

Interspersed throughout the village are a large number of agricultural buildings of four main types: the hay barn (*Scheune*), stall (*Stall*), and two different storage huts, one for food such as meat and cheese as well as for household effects (*Speicher*), and one for grain, which includes a threshing floor (*Stadel*). All of these buildings are made of wood, although some newer stalls have stone walls with a wooden hay barn set on top.

Stalls rarely stand alone in the village, for space is at a premium and the height of a stall is limited by its use, thus allowing for another story to be added on above. They usually do not hold more than four or five cows, each in its own little cubicle. The ceiling is generally not more than six feet high, and there is no ventilation except for a tiny window next to the door. Outside there is an area for collecting manure, which is then used for fertilizer. Within the limits of the village there are over 50 stalls for cattle, sheep, and goats. Stalls for pigs are also common, although they are not as formidable, and therefore are less likely to be combined with another building. Horses and mules, used in the Lötschental before the war, also required stalls, but there were so few of them that they hardly require mention.

Hay barns tend to be combined with stalls, both for the convenience of their complementary functions and because of the premium on land within the village. This is possible since the stall is the sturdiest of the agricultural buildings, and is the only one which can safely take a second story. Thus although there are a few barns that stand alone in the village, none are combined with any other type of building except the stall.

The two types of storage buildings are found both alone and in combination with stalls. Here the combination has nothing to do with the functions of the respective buildings, but rather with the need to use vertical and preserve hori-

A typical barn near the village.

zontal space. Both types of storage building are an extension of the house, which by its size limits the preparation and storage of food.

The *Speicher* is used to keep cheese, bread (particularly before the war when a family baked only once a month in the communal oven), smoked and dried meat, grain after threshing, flour, and grain to be kept for planting the next crop. It could also be used to keep wool which had not yet been spun, various fabrics and special festive clothing, and other miscellaneous possessions which would not fit in the house. It has no windows or other openings, only small slits in the walls to allow enough air in to dry the meat and preserve the other products. If a *Speicher* is owned jointly by more than one household, as is generally the case, each portion is set off inside by a partition and each has a separate door.

Whereas the *Speicher* deals with many aspects of the agricultural operation, the *Stadel* is basically a one-purpose building, serving as a granary. Moreover, its function is limited to a very short period of the agricultural cycle. The *Stadel* consists of a threshing floor and several partitions for storing the grain and straw. It tends to be divided more than other buildings, since the main investment is the threshing floor, and the amount of space needed for such a short time for threshing makes it more economical to have several owners share the cost of construction and maintenance.

One last agricultural building, an isolated example, is the village dairy cooperative (*Sennerei*). This small, stone-walled hut was built in 1932 and housed the necessary equipment for making butter and cheese from the milk delivered by the members of the cooperative. Since the war, however, the cooperative has disbanded and the building is no longer in use.

3 / The village and its inhabitants

DEMOGRAPHY AND CITIZENSHIP

In 1970, the village of Kippel had 462 residents, of whom over 99 percent were Roman Catholic, 100 percent were native German speakers, and over 90 percent were born in the village. Such a remarkable degree of homogeneity is understandable in light of the ecological situation, where the socially defined community tends to be the exclusive occupant of its own valley.

As the figures below indicate, the population of Kippel, and of the entire valley, has grown steadily over the last century:

Year	Kippel	Lötschental
1870	211	922
1880	229	955
1890	240	960
1900	248	999
1910	300	2091*
1920	308	1188
1930	293	1205
1941	340	1375
1950	363	1412
1960	393	1454
1970	462	N.A.

* Includes temporary resident labor camp at Goppenstein, in the commune of Ferden, during the construction of the Lötschberg Tunnel.

The population has more than doubled in the last hundred years, due to a high birth rate, a declining death rate, particularly infant mortality, and a low emigration rate.

The real test of homogeneity lies in the citizenship and place of birth of the residents of the village. Swiss citizenship, or *Bürgerrecht*, is automatically conferred upon all children of any male citizen of a community, and the children of any female who by legal act chooses to retain for her children citizenship in the community where she herself holds such a position. Thus the following figures on citizenship show the high percentage of village residents who are citizens of Kippel.

19

CITIZENSHIP OF VILLAGE RESIDENTS

Year	Total Population	Kippel	Other Valais Commune	Other Canton	Other Country
1900	248	239	9	0	0
1910	300	284	15	1	0
1920	308	285	21	2	0
1930	293	269	20	3	1
1941	340	313	22	5	0
1950	363	335	24	4	0
1960	393	350	33	6	4
1970	462	426	25	7	4

Columns 1 and 2 give the total population of the village in a particular year, while column 3 gives the number out of that total who were citizens of Kippel. The next columns list respectively the number of citizens of other communes in the canton of Valais (primarily the other three villages in the valley), citizens of another canton in Switzerland, and finally those of another country. (The foreign citizens listed in the past two census years consist of the secondary school teacher and his family who were brought in because of the lack of qualified personnel within the village.)

The village of Kippel is technically divided into two separate entities, the municipal community or community of residents, and the corporation of burghers or community of citizens. This dualism dates back to the federal constitution of 1848, and the Valais cantonal constitution of 1852; before 1848 there was only the latter type in Valais (Kämpfen 1942:10). The municipal community is concerned with a territorial principle relating to the people who live within its boundaries, while the corporation of burghers is based upon the old definition of the city as the sum of its citizens (Niederer 1956).

In previous centuries the community of burghers constituted a veritable economic and political corporation, but the federal constitution of 1848 gave each Swiss citizen the right to settle in the canton and community of his choice, and in 1874 free exercise of civic rights in the place of residence was added (Berthoud 1967:201). Citizenship is not bound up with residence or land ownership, but rather with origin. In its present meaning it is a legal and heritable status in relation to the community of origin. Every Swiss citizen is necessarily a citizen of a commune. It is indicative of the political structure of Switzerland that in order to become naturalized as a Swiss citizen a person must first obtain the rights of citizenship in a commune.

Citizenship in the village of Kippel may be obtained either as a birthright if one's parents were citizens of Kippel, or else (for women) by marrying a citizen of Kippel. There is also at least one case of the community granting honorary citizenship to a long-time resident it wished to honor. However, the common method by which an outsider obtains citizenship in a new community, by purchasing it, is impossible in Kippel. A document in the communal archives from 1790 declares that no one may be taken in as a burgher because it has in the past created trouble in the entire valley, since citizenship in two communities confers an unfair advantage upon some individuals. Moreover, henceforth resident noncitizens must pay a fee for residence privileges, apparently since Kippel citizens were dissatisfied that others were entitled to certain privileges without paying. This ruling applies to all who seek citizenship, be they from other villages in the Lötschental, from elsewhere in Switzerland, or from a foreign country.

The function of the resident community is primarily centered around administration and public works, whereas the corporation of burghers is concerned exclusively with those aspects of village life which affect only the citizens, such as the necessary legal administration governing citizenship, or the administration of property owned exclusively by the corporate citizenry (Bachmann 1970:178). In the Lötschental the citizenry of each village holds most of the publicly owned property, and the resident community has only that which is necessary for its end of the administration, such as land for public buildings, streets, and parking areas.

Whereas in a heterogeneous city the different group functions based on the distinction between resident and burgher are more important, in a small, homogeneous village such as Kippel, where the vast majority of residents are citizens, the distinction practically disappears, for the same people are involved in either case and the end result is the same. Thus the village government deals simultaneously with problems technically concerning only one or the other segment of the village, for it is truly representative of both.

Numerous officials are necessary for governing the village, although in Kippel the homogeneity of the residents has enabled the combination of what are normally two bodies—one for the citizenry and one for the residents—into one village council. This council consists of seven men elected by the men of the village. (Women only gained the right to vote in 1969 in the village, and national suffrage did not come until 1971.) Among the members the two highest vote-getters are designated as president and vice-president, respectively, while a third is chosen as secretary on the basis of his qualifications with regard to the specific duties of that office. The village council deals with various problems of administration, such as taxation, transportation, public works, and local projects for the benefit of the village. In addition, there is also a valley council, made up of president and vice-president of each village council plus an additional member who serves as secretary. This group decides on matters affecting the entire valley: the road, public works crossing communal boundaries, school terms, and, in earlier days, the network of irrigation canals extending throughout all four communities.

Several other official positions also exist within the realm of village government. The judge and vice-judge, a three-member advisory council, and a two-member police council all deal with various aspects of social control. A village keeper is in charge of access ways, as well as control over stray animals, primarily sheep and goats in the forests. Another official is in charge of arranging work to be done for the community. He sets up the project, assigns workers, and then directs their payment, much the same as a general contractor. The animal inspector counts and inspects all animals in the village annually. The village auctioneer is in charge of all sales of village property. Two separate officials are in charge of the civil records (vital statistics) and the cadastre, or book of land records. Another is in charge of maintaining the village tools, machinery, etc. A milk-measurer takes samples every month for health inspection and also to measure the fat content, as well as the total amount of milk, which is important today for government subsidies. The schoolhouse custodian doubles as the street cleaner and general village handyman. He is also responsible for seeing that the water system that supplies the village is in repair.

Aside from these individual positions, there are numerous commissions dealing with various aspects of village life. The church council, consisting of the priest, the president, vice-president, chaplain and one other burgher, is charged with caring for the church, keeping it in repair, and handling a variety of related secular problems. The school committee traditionally had three members to deal with school affairs. Today in Kippel there are two such committees, one for the primary and household schools together, and one for the secondary school. The latter committee consists of three members from Kippel and one from each of the other three communities in the Lötschental. The two-member tax commission computes and collects village taxes and pays debts that come from tax funds. The forest committee, consisting of the president, vice-president, village forester, and one other, deals with all problems relating to the forest, primarily gathering wood for construction or fuel and, more recently, the network of roads through the woods as well.

There is surprisingly little duplication of service among the positions of public administration. The village council is, elected every four years, and its composition is usually changed by at least several members. There does not appear to have been a long reign of one person at the head of village government, and the only posts which have been continuously occupied are those which are not particularly influential, yet which require a specific skill and familiarity, such as the forester or the record keepers. Other offices rotate with relative frequency among the men of the village, and only the extremely marginal villagers are excluded from public service.

Many years ago the most important position in the village was the *Gewalthaber*, literally the "holder of power." This official was vested with a wide range of duties and obligations, which the village protocol of 1867 defines as follows:

1. calling the entire community together when necessary
2. administering cultivation, irrigation, and harvest of communal land, and maintaining communal buildings
3. collecting and distributing manure
4. reporting those tardy or absent from communal work projects
5. collecting fines and taxes levied by the community
6. supplying wine when necessary
7. purchasing and caring for the communally owned breeding bull
8. caring for the community and assisting the village council
9. reporting on all activities to the community

For all this the *Gewalthaber* was paid only his expenses, often not even that much. Thus at the end of his one year term in which he had neglected his farming to fulfill the duties of office, he was often heavily in debt. It is not clear whether the term was limited to a year because of the expense, or because of the power and responsibility involved, but in either case this office clearly demanded too much of any one individual. In a society with a wide disparity of wealth it might have been used as a leveling device, but in the relatively economically homogeneous community of Kippel it did not have that effect. Ultimately the office was discarded and the duties distributed among other existing ones. The paid position of schoolhouse custodian was developed, with the additional tasks of maintaining the breeding bull, arranging for supplies for the various festive occasions within the village, and maintaining public works.

KINSHIP AND MARRIAGE

Residents of Kippel belong to 13 separate family groups (*Stämme*), each of which traces itself back to its own common ancestor (*Stammvater*).* There are only nine surnames representing these thirteen groups, for in two cases two, and in one case three groups have the same surname. Although members of these families cannot trace any relationship along descent lines to those nonkin groups with the same name, undoubtedly an earlier tie existed. The creation of separate but similarly named families seems to have occurred after a long interval during which a branch of the original family resided in a different village from the main stem, thus severing its tie. A member of that branch ultimately migrated within the valley to a village where members of the main stem resided. If enough time had elapsed so that the common ancestor was forgotten and, more important, so that the relationship between members of the groups was not close enough to prohibit marriage, then the groups began to think of themselves as unrelated.

It is difficult to determine the familial makeup of the population of Kippel in the distant past, but it is certain that it has changed and continues to change rather rapidly. Several family names have disappeared from Kippel within the last generation, while other families have greatly increased in number. This can be due to a variety of unrelated factors, such as extensive migration, a large proportion of females in one generation, few males marrying and remaining in the village, childless marriages, or more likely a combination of all of these. In Kippel as of my census date, January 1, 1970, there were five family groups out of thirteen with only one married male presently residing in the village. Although each of the five has male children (not yet of marriageable age), which indicates that each family name will most likely persist at least into the next generation, still this example shows how easy it is for a family to disappear from the village rolls within a very short time.

---

* Excluding nonnative residents, such as the schoolteacher and clergymen, who comprise less than 3 percent of the village population.

Descent is bilateral, with a very slight emphasis upon the male side. A child takes his father's last name as his own, and never uses the mother's maiden name, not even as a middle name. However, a married woman will frequently append her maiden name to her married surname, especially in formal circumstances or to distinguish herself from another woman with the same name. The name then appears hyphenated, first her Christian name, then husband's surname-hyphen-maiden surname.

As a result of having so few family groups in the population, there is an extremely intricate network of relations connecting all villagers with one another. Large families and a high rate of endogamy also contribute to this network. No distinctions are made as to whether relatives such as aunts, uncles, or cousins are patrilateral or matrilateral, at least not in the kinship terminology. The same terms are applied to both father's brother and mother's brother, likewise father's brother's son and mother's brother's son, as well as mother's sister's son, etc. In fact, the only distinction that is not directly comparable to common English usage in the United States is that between a female cousin and a male cousin, but there is still a broader term which can be used to refer to a cousin of either sex. Only first cousins are addressed by these terms for cousin, and further relationships are not accorded a special term. People generally recognize that a distant relationship exists, but since it does not have any bearing upon marriage prohibition (first cousin or closer), it has no significance. If, however, two distant relatives are members of the same family group this fact will also be recognized, but again there is no special term for such a relationship; instead it will be explained by a phrase such as "we are from the same *Stamm*."

To get an idea of the extent of the kinship network, I once made a tally of all the relatives of one young man of marriageable age. Both his parents were born in Kippel and came from rather large families, so that while it is not a random choice, it does indicate the potential degree of relationship of members of the community. A count of those relatives within the degree of kinship which would eliminate them as marriage partners (i.e. through first cousin) yields a total of 63 villagers. When the categories of first cousin once removed (first cousins of ego's parents or children of ego's first cousins) and second cousin (children of first cousins who are not siblings) are included, the total rises to 125, or over one-quarter of the entire village.

This tally indeed emphasizes the range of the kinship network within the village. It is even more astounding when we consider that except for aunts and uncles, it does not show affinal relations, for example, the husband or wife of cousins or siblings. In some cases the same person appears twice on one tally; that is, he or she is related to both the mother and father of the young man in the example. These cases have been screened from the tally so as not to increase the figures artificially, but they illustrate yet another aspect of the intricate web of kinship ties that bind the villagers together. In the case of the young man in question, including affinals he is related to about a third of the population of the village within the range of second cousin.

There is no uniform code of behavior toward kinsmen, other than the general expectation that the communalism and mutual aid existing among all villagers be at least as strong among them. Cooperation among households more often than not is based upon a tie of kinship, but upon no specific tie, that is, it could just as likely be brother–brother as father-in-law—son-in-law. Kinship ties play an important role in new ventures, in that when an innovator decides upon a new project beyond his means he usually turns to a relative rather than a random villager. Of course a major reason for this is grounded in the inheritance system, which creates strong economic ties between siblings or affinals.

In general, however, there is not a noticeable degree of difference in behavior toward relatives and nonrelatives in daily life within the village. Arguments and animosities are just as likely to occur among kinsmen as not, not only concerning inheritance disputes but even petty quarrels over minor incidents. In-law relationships tend to be noted, and the terms for brother-in-law and sister-in-law are preferred in normal speech to simple use of names, but again there is little difference in actual behavior except under special circumstances where more than just the normal degree of cooperation is required.

Of course, occasions arise when certain individuals are singled out for special treatment, and on such occasions kinship plays an important role. Perhaps the best example is that of life crisis rites, such as baptism, marriage, or death. Here special roles are usually assigned to one or more kinsmen, be it godparent at a baptism, witness at a wedding, or pallbearer at a funeral. In no case is it obligatory that a relative be chosen, however.

Fictive kinship in this egalitarian society, already infused with a tight net of interrelations, does not play the same role as in more highly stratified peasant societies typical of the Mediterranean region. Reciprocation is already guaranteed under the system, and its reinforcement through ritual godparenthood is superfluous. It can perhaps be seen as a reminder of the potential obligations among kinsmen, but in no case does it create new roles or new expectations. Godparenthood and other such positions seem to be primarily important in a religious sense, in that they confer a special honor upon the recipient through their participation in a religious ceremony.

There is a high rate of endogamy or marriage within both the village and especially the valley. Out of a total of 226 marriages since 1900 involving at least one resident of Kippel, 152 or 67 percent were valley endogamous and 81 of those were village endogamous as well. Furthermore, we find that a patrilocal residence rule reigns. The new couple tends to settle in the man's village, either in the house of his father or, as is becoming increasingly the case, in a new apartment or house. The rate of valley endogamy was even higher prior to the second world war, for emigration was fairly low until after the war. Thus if we consider the 99 marriages which occurred between 1900–1940, we find that 72 were valley endogamous, of which 39 were also village endogamous. We need only recall the example of the kinship network of the young man cited earlier to get the full force of these percentages. At the same time that endogamous marriages are hampered by the intricate kinship network that severely limits eligible marriage partners, they work to reinforce it and extend it even further.

Rarely does an outsider marry into Kippel. In just over 2 percent of the cases has a man brought in an outsider as his bride, and never has an outside (non-Lötschental) man settled in Kippel with his local bride. On the contrary, in 93.2 percent of the marriages involving an outsider (30.5 percent of the total number of marriages involving someone from Kippel) the couple settled outside the valley. This does not mean that the men from Kippel emigrated to their spouse's village after marriage, but more likely that the new (neolocal) household was set up in the city or town where the man found work. Of course it is not unlikely that a man first settled down outside the valley and then married a local girl in his new place of residence. It should be pointed out, however, that there are considerable problems in exogamous marriages in Kippel, primarily economic ones. As Berthoud says, "The remarkable cohesion of the community and close interdependence of families explain the total level of territorial endogamy" (1967:75).

It would be untrue to claim that it is not difficult for an outsider to break into Kippel society, even a woman from another Lötschental village. The tight network of kinship and mutual aid binds the people together, and an outsider is seen as having no investment in this network, and therefore fewer ties with the natives of the village. For a non-Lötschental woman to marry into Kippel is even more difficult, for she encounters many strange customs, not to mention a new dialect. Certainly there is tremendous social pressure upon a young man to marry a local girl, at least a valley girl, if he plans to remain in Kippel.

But there is an even more important pressure for endogamy, an economic pressure tied in with the rule of inheritance. Bachmann claims that an individual's holding before marriage (assuming he has inherited anything at all) is usually not enough to support a family, and this is a major cause of endogamy. Even if it is enough to support a family, it probably is not enough to care for future heirs (1970:251).

Of course, it should be noted that for Blatten (the community where Bachmann made his study) this problem is more severe than for the other three villages of the Lötschental, since it is so far away from them. If, for example, a girl from Ferden married a man from Blatten and subsequently moved there, she would have to rent her land in Ferden or else trade or sell it so as to be able to have land near Blatten. However, if this same girl from Ferden were to marry into Kippel or even Wiler, this problem would not exist, and she could easily keep her land in Ferden without great hardship (see map p. xi). Thus in the case of Blatten which Bachmann describes, we could expect an even higher rate of village endogamy at the expense of marriages with residents of the other villages of the Lötschental.

One result of the longstanding practice of endogamy is a relatively high rate of intermarriage and inbreeding. Although the law of the Roman Catholic church prohibits first cousin marriage, there have been occasions when the church has allowed it, usually accompanied by the payment of a special tax. Traditionally, such marriages were frequently made by nobility throughout Europe in an effort to consolidate power and maintain family estates intact. For this reason, among others, the church banned them, or at least levied a tax against them to prevent inbreeding from becoming commonplace. This tax applies in Kippel, although the situation is reversed, in that consolidation of power or land is not served by inbreeding specifically, but only by village or valley endogamy.

Marriage of relatives beyond the degree of first cousin is a fairly common occurrence. While no scientific study has been made to determine the effects of inbreeding within the valley, the villagers are themselves aware of the possibility of congenital diseases and hereditary weaknesses being transmitted and compounded through marriage of close relatives. This awareness, however, is relatively recent in its effects upon actual choice of a marriage partner, and therefore the effects of increasing exposure to the outside world (and thereby to a greater number of potential mates) must be put forth as a major factor in the decline of intermarriage. Nonetheless, today there are several large families in which two or more siblings share the same congenital malady.

Marriage in the Lötschental occurs at a relatively late age, as indicated by the figures below:

	1900–1924	1925–1949	1950–1959	1960–1969
Average age of male	32.3	31.0	30.7	27.1
Average age of female	29.0	29.5	27.5	26.0

Especially in the prewar era when the agro-pastoral economy reigned, marriage was frequently put off until one or both partners had come into part or all of their inheritance, for since there was no dowry or bride price, the couple could not make a living and at the same time remain independent. It was not always necessary to have a separate house or apartment, for if one or both of the husband's parents were still alive the new couple would probably live with them. The important thing was to have security, to be economically independent. Occasionally, if a son wanted to marry, his father might give him a cow and use-rights to enough land that he would be able to live off the yield plus what he could afford to rent. The rest of his inheritance would come at the father's death.

An interesting result of the late age of marriage is the pattern of courtship. The church, through the resident clergyman, imposed strict controls over the interaction of young unmarried men and women and, as in every society, they found ways to get around these limitations. In the summer, when the young girls were temporarily relocated on the summer pastures for the purpose of tending the cattle, boys would walk up from the village in the evening and knock on the window of the huts where the girls they were courting stayed. Then in a rather stereotyped fashion the boy would sing in a disguised voice, telling of his love and devotion. If the girl were so inclined, she would let the young man into the hut and serve him a snack of milk and cheese. As Siegen notes, "There are many tales told of secret merrymakings and dances in the alp-huts" (1960:52).

Another common courtship pattern, also tied in with the economic cycle, took place during the winter when the cattle were located in the stalls near the village. The task of milking, feeding, and tending the cattle was generally allocated to young girls. Since the girls went alone to the stalls, it presented a perfect opportunity for young men to accompany them and thus escape parental supervision. An expression in the local dialect describes the pattern of courting— "gah' helfi hirtu," meaning to go help tend the animals. Predictably, once the couple is married the man ceases to accompany his wife to the stall, raising the question of how much he ever really helped.

Once a couple has settled upon each other, the courtship frequently lasts ten years or longer before they wed. It is not uncommon for a boy and girl to start courting in their teens, yet the average age of marriage would indicate that most wait at least until their late twenties to marry. This suggests that if the courtship develops before the age of marriage is reached, there is less pressure to marry than if it had developed later. The couple becomes accustomed to the situation long before it can possibly be changed. Moreover, it has been suggested that courtship might serve as a sort of security; that is, if a boy or girl knows that there is always going to be someone there waiting, there is less pressure to go out and get someone, which in turn would involve pressure toward marriage.*

Late marriage, at least for women, has also resulted from an attempt to limit family size. In this strict Roman Catholic community, artificial means of birth control were unknown until recently, and large families were commonplace. By waiting until half the child-bearing period was past before marrying, women were able to control the number of children they had. Nevertheless, large families were the rule, averaging 5.7 children in the second quarter of this century and almost 5 children for marriages between 1950–1959.

With such large families being the rule rather than the exception, obviously some means of population control must exist if the inheritance system and other aspects of the social structure vulnerable to population pressure are to be maintained. Emigration was a relatively minor factor, due primarily to the strength of the ties of kinship and mutual assistance, along with the partible inheritance which gave everyone land and buildings within the Lötschental. Artificial birth control was not practiced before the war, and child mortality was not high enough to exert a major influence on controlling the population.

Another factor emerges in the battle against population pressure within a limited environment, namely celibacy. Large numbers of people either chose or were forced to remain unmarried. Moreover, in the event of an early death, the surviving spouse almost never remarried. In Kippel in 1970, according to my personal census, there were 45 single residents over forty years of age, 17 between thirty and forty years old, and another 17 over twenty-five, for a total of 79 individuals above the expected age of marriage. This figure represents over a third (34.5 percent) of the 229 villagers over the age of twenty-five. Even if we consider that marriage occurs in many cases later than age twenty-five, we still find a surprisingly high percentage of the population unmarried. Of the total population over forty years of age (154 individuals), 45 or 29.2 percent never married.

What were the forces that caused such a high rate of celibacy? In one sense

---

* I am indebted to Professor Harry Levy for suggesting this idea.

the puritanical teachings of the church, placing a positive value on virginity and a negative value on sexuality, sex education, and outward display of sexual prowess, even after marriage, all helped to maintain a high rate of celibacy. Yet this must be countered by the folk view, particularly of the women, that bearing children is a prerequisite for salvation. Old spinsters are frequently heckled by the taunts of young children, "You'll go to hell, because you don't have any children." Certainly the teachings of the church regarding family life and the responsibility of the parishioners to increase the following also must be considered as a positive factor in favor of marriage. Religion, it would seem, cannot account alone for the unmarried segment of the population.

Rather, it seems to have been primarily an economic consideration. When an inheritance is divided, the estate of a childless heir reverts to his or her siblings upon that person's death. Thus if a man had ten children, all of whom married and themselves had children, his estate would be divided into tenths and no child would receive any substantial amount for himself. On the other hand, if this man could somehow see to it that only one or two of his children married, the entire estate would ultimately go only to those children, although the others would in effect have use-rights to their share while they lived. In this way, a man could provide for future generations by limiting the number of final actual divisions of his estate.

Pressure did not necessarily always come from the parent, but sometimes also from siblings. If a group of siblings pooled their inheritance because the estate had not been large enough to divide, then obviously future divisions would have to be avoided. However, a member of this group could not marry without demanding his share of the estate to support his future family. In such a case, the siblings could exert pressure upon each other to prevent marriage and the breakup of the commonly owned estate, and indeed this was often the case. What might be enough land for three if worked jointly is not necessarily enough for two plus one if worked separately.

A final possibility is that long courtships contributed to the high rate of celibacy within the village. It is not unlikely that after ten, fifteen, or even twenty years of courting in which there is no sexual activity of any major import, it sometimes ceases to be an important drive toward marriage. If, on the other hand, there is incidence of sexual activity during courtship, the pressure toward marriage is likewise very low. If a pregnancy occurs, then the couple marries. But if none occurs, chances are there will be no marriage. Then, too, if a courtship lasts into the thirties and then is broken off, it might be difficult for the individuals to start up another one. A lack of suitable marriage partners would then force them to remain single.

It should perhaps be noted that a high rate of unmarried individuals is characteristic of the entire canton of Valais, and is not merely a peculiarity of Kippel. Loup claims that while celibacy is caused by overpopulation and the difficult life of a woman in a mountain agro-pastoral household, another major factor is the desire to conserve wealth, leading to fewer marriages because of the partible inheritance practiced there (1965:178).

DIET

The subsistence-oriented economy of the Lötschental has never been able to provide all the dietary necessities for the inhabitants of the valley. Grapes will not grow as high up as the valley floor, and the nature of the passage to the lower wine-producing region in the Rhone Valley is such that frequent commuting is impossible. In this respect the Lötschental is unlike other lateral valleys in Valais, such as Embd in the Vispertal, where vineyards are situated near the village itself (Imboden 1956:42), or Val d'Anniviers, where easy transit allows many people to move down into the Rhone Valley for a period during the summer to harvest the vineyards they own there (Dumont 1954: chapter 8).

The climate in the Lötschental, combined with the rugged terrain, forced the residents to supplement their grain supplies as well. Few families owned enough arable land of high enough quality that the yield from their fields would suffice. Other nonlocal products were also purchased from outside the valley, primarily coffee, tobacco, sugar, and salt. Before the completion of the railroad line through the Lötschberg, men used to make the long trek down to the Rhone Valley, sometimes as far away as the market town of Sion, to purchase or trade for necessities which they would then haul back by mule. Once the railroad was built, it became a relatively simple matter to have products shipped into Goppenstein, from which they could be brought into the valley with comparative ease.

The mainstays of the traditional Lötschental diet are potatoes, bread, and dairy products. The potato crop has always been sufficient to feed the population of the valley and some animals as well. During the Depression the potato was the only thing that saved the valley from starvation. One woman recalled that her family was so poor that if they had some cheese to put on their potatoes at dinner they considered themselves fortunate. Bread was out of the question— potatoes and milk kept them alive and healthy. As another informant put it, "A diet of potatoes four times a day might not seem very pleasant, but at least everyone had enough to eat." No one died of starvation, and only a few were damaged by malnutrition, so the valley is thankful for its good fortune during this critical period.

Bread baked from local or imported rye is another staple in the Lötschental diet. Until 1920 there was no bakery in the valley, and all bread was baked in the communal ovens located in every village or hamlet. Each family would bake once a month, and the rye bread was well suited to this schedule, for it kept well and was eaten (actually preferred) in a very hard state. The construction of a bakery in Kippel marks the beginning of the change from rye to white bread, a change that proceeded only gradually until after the war. Even in the more prosperous times the local grain supplies did not suffice for the entire village. About 200 hours of labor for fertilizing, tilling, planting, and harvesting are reckoned for a yield of 50 kilograms (110 pounds) of grain, and at this rate the labor force was simply inadequate to provide enough grain for itself. Nevertheless the villagers strove to grow as much as possible, and the lower fields were devoted almost exclusively to grain rather than hay.

The Lötschental is not noted for its cheese, and in fact one never sees it on the market outside the valley. It is a dry, low-fat cheese which does not keep well, because it is made after the cream is skimmed off for butter; what little is made is quickly consumed by the owner. Imported cheese has become more important in the diet since the construction of the railroad, although it was not until after the war that people could afford to give up their own cheese making entirely.

The most important dairy product in the valley is milk. A fair estimate would be that the average family consumes at least a quart per person per day, either straight or with coffee, sometimes even in a pudding. Since milk is essential to survival, those villagers without cows or goats (or with an insufficient number to feed their household) must find a way to supplement their milk supply. In the prewar days of the agricultural economy when cash was not always available to purchase needed food, milk became the most important factor in cooperative arrangements among families in the village. A poorer villager would help out a wealthier one (usually a relative, if possible) regularly throughout the year by performing various agricutural tasks, and in return he would be paid a daily ration of milk. In this way even the poorest man could feed his family if he had enough land to grow potatoes and enough strength to work for others who then paid him in milk. Lacking cows, he could even harvest and sell the hay from the rest of his land and raise enough cash or credit to provide the other bare essentials for his family.

Another common arrangement was that if someone had an extra building or land that he could not work, he could turn it over to a relative in return for payment in milk. This was especially popular among older persons who wanted to give up agriculture but had no way of supporting themselves if they did not belong to a large household. Such a person could give up his entire holding of hay fields and barns in return for milk and a few other products and still retain enough land to grow potatoes and grain, a less demanding activity.

Also important in the diet, but to a lesser extent, is meat. Daily consumption of meat is uncommon in the Lötschental, and even the Sunday meat dish is not consistent, since it depends upon the time of year and wealth of the family. Mutton is the most common meat, certainly more important than beef. Cows are only slaughtered when they cannot be sold, while sheep are raised specifically for the meat they provide, along with their wool. Pigs are also raised exclusively for meat, and although a swine count is difficult because of the seasonal nature of the slaughter, traditionally most households probably slaughtered at least one pig at the beginning of each winter.

Meat is preserved by salting it and then letting it hang in the *Speicher* to dry. Often it is first hung in the chimney to give it a smoked flavor and ensure the initial drying. It keeps this way for a year or more, so that a household can slaughter an animal and dry the meat for consumption without fear of it spoiling. This would appear to make slaughtering an affair for each household individually, but such is not the case. On the contrary, it is common to share an animal after slaughtering it; if it is a small animal, such as a sheep or a pig, it could be divided among several siblings or distributed to married children, while a cow would probably be divided into quarters or halves and would be sold or exchanged with another family on a reciprocal basis.

Fruit was never an important item in the Lötschental diet. The climate is partially to blame for this, but an equally important factor is the resistance of the villagers to dietary innovation and change. Vegetables are grown on a small scale within the valley and, like fruit, there is little mention of any importation of large quantities from outside until recently. The vegetables grown in household gardens are enough to supplement the diet, but not to become a staple in themselves. Other additions to the diet, such as nuts or wild berries, are almost totally lacking.

The common practice in the Lötschental is to eat four or five times during the day—at least this is the traditional practice of the agriculturalists which has been carried over to the present, although the factory workers have had to adjust their meals to their work schedules. Breakfast is served before the workday begins and usually consists of bread and cheese, with coffee and milk. Occasionally another meal, or more accurately a snack, is eaten in the morning at nine or ten, but it would be something brought out to the fields to tide the workers over until lunch. The midday meal is served around noon and is the major meal of the day. It includes soup of some sort, with vegetables occasionally added. Potatoes are eaten either in the soup or separately, in the latter case supplemented by cheese. Meat is added to the soup when possible, but for most families this means only on Sundays and festive occasions. The evening meal is served at about four o'clock, again either in the fields or at home depending upon the season. It consists of cheese and bread, with either coffee and milk or wine. The last meal is eaten before retiring, usually a thick milk or soup along with cheese and bread or boiled potatoes.

This schedule of meals is of course idealized, describing the traditionally most common and often most preferred diet. The amount eaten is not excessive, and is always tempered by the current economic conditions. It is merely spread out over a greater number of meals. Tea made from local herbs is sometimes served at meals, although it is generally reserved for medicinal purposes. Occasionally baked goods will be added to a festive meal, but otherwise the menu varies little from day to day, or even from meal to meal.

Heavy use of alcoholic beverages is not uncommon in the Lötschental. Beer was never as important as wine, for not only is wine more potent, it is also more readily available. Transportation difficulties dictate the predominance of wine for both these reasons. The most popular sort, a white wine called *fendant*, is the major product of Valais vineyards.

Wine is drunk mostly at public houses, less frequently and in lesser amounts at home. Only men patronize these establishments regularly, although women sometimes accompany their husbands on Sunday after church. Alcoholism is a common problem, formerly a seasonal one, but not to the extent that it is in some other European peasant societies. The lack of money was perhaps the prime limiting factor here, for the villagers were forced to buy almost all the alcohol they consumed. This led to a situation whereby aside from a few chronic alcoholics, the main use of wine was at communal festivals, where overindulgence was often the case. Between festivals, consumption depended upon income and opportunity; those with continual access to alcohol, primarily tavern keepers, exhibited a high rate of alcoholism.

Beer was traditionally a summer drink, for it could only be brought into the valley during the summer and could not be kept as long as wine, nor would it last long once the keg was opened. A few people still make alcoholic drinks themselves, either wine from a local source such as the hawthorn berry, or else *schnaps*, a generic term for any type of strong fruit brandy. *Kirsch*, or cherry brandy, and apple brandy are the most common forms, along with a schnaps made from wild flowers. Absinthe, although outlawed since the beginning of this century, is also available and even locally manufactured in small amounts.

COMMUNICATION

Until the construction of the Lötschberg Railway, mail service to the Lötschental was through Gampel in the Rhone Valley, and the postman had to make the long trek down and back with a mule to haul the mail. After the railroad was built, mail was delivered to Goppenstein and from there it could be brought into the valley more easily. Thus, the climatic limitations on contact with the outside were lessened, for transportation to and from Goppenstein was made possible throughout most of the year. But communication with the outside world was never considered a major problem in the Lötschental, for until the war there was no pressing need to be in constant close contact. With an agricultural economy bordering on self-sufficiency, and the general availability of goods shipped by rail into the valley, the limiting factor was not communication but income.

Communication within the valley, and particularly within the village, is much more important for the prewar period. Although literacy has been known in the Lötschental for over 600 years, not until this century has it approached totality. In spite of the high degree of literacy throughout much of the history of the valley, other means of communication have developed which have superseded written records and procedures. Means of identification have been developed to cope with situations that require a more permanent form of communication or recordkeeping.

One of the more common and widely used forms of identification is the house-sign, or more precisely the household sign. Each family and each independent adult has a separate sign that is used for identification and indirectly symbolizes membership in the community. The signs are simple figures, sometimes even letters of the alphabet. Numerous variations on any one letter or figure are possible as well. Some examples are given on page 34, along with the dialect term for them and a translation (cf. Anneler 1917, Stebler 1907). These household signs are carved into wood and used for various purposes. When a task requires communal labor, but not the entire community, separate pieces of wood, each with the house-

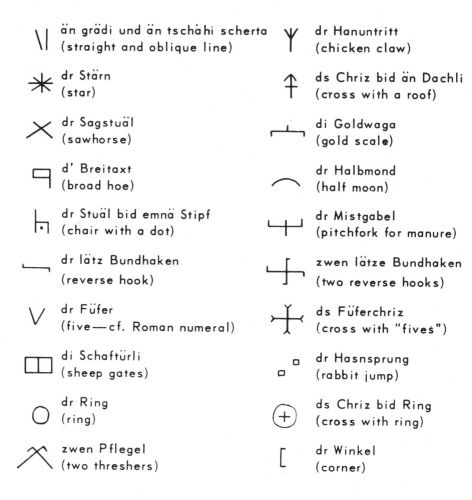

än grädi und än tschähi scherta
(straight and oblique line)

dr Stärn
(star)

dr Sagstuäl
(sawhorse)

d' Breitaxt
(broad hoe)

dr Stuäl bid emnä Stipf
(chair with a dot)

dr lätz Bundhaken
(reverse hook)

dr Füfer
(five—cf. Roman numeral)

di Schaftürli
(sheep gates)

dr Ring
(ring)

zwen Pflegel
(two threshers)

dr Hanuntritt
(chicken claw)

ds Chriz bid än Dachli
(cross with a roof)

di Goldwaga
(gold scale)

dr Halbmond
(half moon)

dr Mistgabel
(pitchfork for manure)

zwen lätze Bundhaken
(two reverse hooks)

ds Füferchriz
(cross with "fives")

dr Hasnsprung
(rabbit jump)

ds Chriz bid Ring
(cross with ring)

dr Winkel
(corner)

sign of one family, are put into a hat and they are drawn one at a time until the required number of workers is chosen. Each household drawn must then supply one man for the task.

In early summer when the number of cows each member of the community will take to the alpine pasture is determined, house-signs carved into wood (*Tesseln*) are used. There are three sets of *Tesseln* used in this procedure: one records the *Alppfund*, the fee that entitles a member to make use of the alp. The household sign of each member is kept in a chest and, since this fee is heritable, the record is permanent. The second set is for the *Krautgeld*, a record of who is actually taking how many cows up to the alp that summer. For each participating member there is a separate piece of wood with his house sign, and at one end notches are carved indicating the number of use-rights he is employing. These are then strung together and are later used to determine the rotation of herding duties on the alp, the obligation passing from one man to another according to position on the string of *Tesseln*. The third set is used to record actual use-rights on the alp, whether used or not. A string of wooden pieces marked with numbers indicating membership in the association that owns the pasture corresponds to the records in the alp book. A corner of each piece is cut out, and goes to the holder of that use-right. The size of the right is recorded on both portions of each piece of wood by means of various lengths and thicknesses of notches, and when the missing piece is put next to its mate these notches match. In this manner the association controls the use of the alp by requiring members to present their *Tesseln* each summer before they may take their animals to the pasture, thus preventing anyone from carving in notches to increase his indicated number of use-rights.

What is so interesting about the use of notches, house-signs, and other nonliterate means of recordkeeping and identification is that even when they are combined with a literate method, such as the alp book, it is the nonliterate form

Old men at the alp reckoning. (Photo by Albert Nyfeler, courtesy of Professor Arnold Niederer)

that is considered the final authority. If the *Tesseln* do not coincide with the book, then the latter is wrong. This is clearly an ingenious way of protecting the illiterate villager from a tyranny by his more educated neighbor, and the fact that it is still in practice shows how effective it has been.

There are yet other uses for the household signs. They are carved into trees to be cut down to designate the future owner of the wood, if that has in fact been predetermined. They can be branded on animals, although this is rarely practiced any more, the preferred method at least for smaller animals being a unique series of notches in the ear. The use of a string or series of *Tesseln* to determine a rotation also comes in handy for regulating the use of irrigation canals. Each member of an irrigation association has one piece of wood, and when all are strung together an order is established.

One of the most ingenious uses of this form of communication is the "fire watch" stake, a long wooden bar with about 80 house-signs carved on it. Each night one person in the village is responsible for the fire watch, which means he has to walk around the village after dark to make sure there is no fire or danger of one. The next day another person is responsible. To see that this duty is equally distributed, the signs of all households in the village are carved in the bar, and after each person has fulfilled his obligation he takes it to the next person whose sign is adjacent to his own on the stake. Theoretically the "fire watch" stake, and thereby also the duty, makes one complete round of the village every 80 days or so, depending upon the exact number of signs carved in it.

This method of communication is similar to the Swedish tradition of the *budkavle*, a symbol of the village which was sent around from one farmstead to another to call a meeting. Here, the settlement pattern decreed a different purpose for the same type of instrument, for in a dispersed settlement such as is common in Sweden, it is important to spread the labor of communication among all involved, while in a nucleated village where actual communication is not a problem, it can be used more as a means of recordkeeping.

House-signs are heritable in the Lötschental. However, if there is more than one child, the sign usually goes to the oldest or the youngest son, the oldest if the father dies before he marries, the youngest if he is still in the household but his brothers have already married when the sign is handed down. Each of the other sons, upon setting up a new household, must have a different sign. Most choose some sort of variation on their father's sign to facilitate identification,

Fire watch stake, with carved house-signs.

for as the fire watch stake indicates, the number of house-signs would be unmanageable if there were not some similarity among those for related heads of households.

Other forms of communication in the village are more or less standard. Most important announcements are made in church at high mass on Sunday, that being the occasion when most villagers are together in the same place at the same time. Announcements may also be written and posted on the bulletin board outside the church. In an emergency or for prearranged activities, the church bells toll in a certain way to call the villagers together or to inform them of an event. There are different patterns that the bells toll in order to announce a church service, a mass, funeral, or to call the villagers together for communal work or any emergency.

Perhaps the most efficient form of communication is gossip. Though not limited to women, gossip is for the most part a female activity, blending in well with the pattern of communal labor and cooperation prevalent in the village. Before the coming of electricity, women used to gather at the fountains to do their laundry and at the communal ovens to bake their bread. They fed their animals at the same time each day, and their work schedules were generally similar enough to allow them to gossip freely about anything and everything. The men, on the other hand, tend to find much of their conversation in the taverns in the village and through frequent roadside conversations or discussions in the fields.

Gossip is efficient in that it ensures rapid transmission of information to a maximum number of people in a minimum amount of time. As one woman proudly proclaimed: "If the doctor is called to someone in the night, by the next morning everyone knows about it." It works to hold the community together, letting nothing escape public knowledge, but at the same time it excludes outsiders from full participation in village life. Lacking participation in the gossip network, an outsider has no way of knowing what goes on in the daily life of the village, and therefore cannot take part in many activities.

Other more sophisticated forms of mass media communication have only become important in the Lötschental in recent years. However, in the time since the war, radio and newspapers have seen widespread distribution, and television, finally arriving in 1970, promises to have a major impact on life in the valley.

THE CHURCH

The sharing of strong religious feelings and participation in an ancient religious tradition is yet another bond among the mountain people of Kippel. They are proud of the history of the church in their village, dating back to 1233 when the Priorate of the Lötschental was established. The church now standing in Kippel was built in the sixteenth century and contains many relics that are likewise centuries old. The parish archives located in the church at Kippel contain printed works almost 500 years old, and all villagers are aware of their existence, although few have read them.

Until 1899 all four communes in the Lötschental belonged to one parish, with the central church being located in Kippel. Blatten broke off first, not surprisingly because of its isolation from the other three villages. Wiler and Ferden remained in the same parish with Kippel until 1956. Although Kippel has always been the religious center of the valley, its importance did not extend significantly into other areas, in that it never became a permanent market center, nor has there ever been a permanent seat of administration located there for the entire valley. So the social bond created through the religious centralization in Kippel has not extended to other aspects of life, and while it did until 1956 maintain ties

Young boys who have just received their first communion.

between the three lower villages, the primary effect was upon only the residents of Kippel.

The Lötschental is 98.7 percent Roman Catholic, but what is more important, the inhabitants are very religious people. In Kippel church attendance is high, with almost every villager attending services at least once each week. They have a saying for this, their *Sonntagspflicht*, or Sunday obligation. Every religious

Young women following a mass celebrating the Immaculate Conception.

The priests saying a blessing at an outdoor altar on Corpus Christi.

holiday requiring church attendance is called "Sunday," regardless of the day of the week it falls on.

Religious activity is not limited to one day of the week, but is an important part of most villagers' daily lives. Aside from the three masses, one rosary and one vesper service on Sunday, there is a morning mass and an evening rosary each day. Formal outings occur with relative frequency, particularly on the many religious holidays celebrated in some fashion within the village. Organized pilgrimages to various chapels in the Lötschental and elsewhere are popular as well, particularly among women.

Informal religious observance, ranging from a casual stop at a roadside cross to a regular visit to an out-of-the-way chapel in the woods, are of major importance to almost every individual in the congregation. Each person has developed over the years various preferences and has personalized the relationship to a particular chapel, either because of the patron saint of the chapel, or for any one of a number of other reasons. Visits to the cemetery to place flowers on a grave and pray for a deceased relative or loved one are favored by many people. Placing incense on the grave, or lighting candles in a chapel is also common. But the most astounding feat occurred in 1940, when Prior Siegen of Kippel and eight of his parishioners climbed the 13,000 foot Bietschhorn,

Old men carry the church relics in religious parades.

carrying a huge wooden cross which they erected on the summit, and then held a mass.

The influence of the church upon the lives of the villagers is immeasurable. The sermons are strict and forceful, and the fact that the priest lives among his parishioners gives him even more opportunity to influence their daily activities. Children are given religious training by the local priest at an early age, and the effect of a tight-knit community exerting pressures toward church attendance means that this training continues for a lifetime. There is not a single important communal occasion where a blessing of some sort is not said, or where religious ritual is not present. Clearly the pattern of cooperation and mutual aid, the bonds of kinship and the multitude of economic and other associations reinforce over and over again the corporateness of the community. Religion creates yet another tie among all villagers; it is certainly of comparable importance in the social realm of village life to the tradition of mutual assistance in the economic realm.

A body of folklore has grown up around many aspects of the religious life typical of the Lötschental. Stories have been popular for many years, and have been collected for this region in numerous volumes. One thing they all have in common is a reference to spirits of some sort and fear of the unknown. These traits are not uncommon even today. Of course villagers exhibit a wide range of temperaments, but there are individuals who avoid walking past the cemetery at night, just as they avoid passing a particular chapel or other building. There have been cases where houses have even been said to be haunted, and in one case in another village in the valley such a house was sold to an outsider for a ridiculously low price because no one from the valley wanted it. Generally the feeling seems to be that spirits, whether related to nature in some way or linked with a religious figure, are harmless unless they are disturbed. They can work in a person's favor by interceding in a crisis, which frequently accounts for a person's acquisition of a particular patron saint. Prayers to a patron figure are a common source of relief from a pressing problem, and in many cases a gift, often a votive picture placed in that saint's chapel, is offered in gratitude.

The heavy reliance upon religion for spiritual support and the frequency of fear of the unknown and of spirits are understandable in light of the physical environment in which the Lötschentalers find themselves. The individual is powerless to subdue his surroundings, and although the community together can manage, it is not without tremendous loss of time, effort, and even life to the random forces of nature. The frustration and powerlessness of the entire community is in this sense expressed in the folklore that emphasizes the capriciousness of unknown beings. The church, through its teachings and practices, reaffirms that it is the community, in this case the religious community acting together, that can survive. At the same time that the individual is directed toward salvation, he is also directed toward the maintenance of the group, the faithful congregation upon whom the tenuous balance rests.

4 / Traditional agro-pastoralism

LAND USE

Just as the agro-pastoral life of an alpine community requires extreme specialization of building types, as has been described for the village of Kippel, a similar specialization of land is necessitated by the ecological factors involved in winning a living from this harsh environment. The type of mixed agriculture and pastoralism practiced in this and other alpine valleys requires considerable diversification, and consequently land must be used in many ways. Add to this the differences in altitude, temperature, exposure to sunshine, and other results of the interplay of ecological elements, and it becomes clear that with the shortage of land in such physically limited surroundings, a system must be developed whereby each person can maximize his own economic operation. Of course, once this system is developed it must be perpetuated, and this is indeed one of the more interesting aspects of traditional alpine life, which will be discussed under the headings of ownership and inheritance.

There are four basic types of agriculture land in Kippel: grassland too poor to yield a hay cutting and therefore used only for grazing (*Weide*); hay fields, which can sometimes be grazed after the hay has been harvested (*Wiese*); cultivated fields planted with grain and potatoes (*Ackerland*); and garden plots (*Garten*).

Garden plots are usually situated in the village, not only because they require so much attention, but also because the land on the valley floor is the richest and the vegetables grown in the gardens are the most delicate of the crops found in the Lötschental. Gardens tend to be quite small, occasionally less than 100 square feet, but rarely more than 1000 square feet, or about 1/40 of an acre. Because gardens contribute a basic subsistence item, each household in the village has one or more plots, or else at least an arrangement with another household to trade some other product for garden vegetables, including cabbage, lettuce, spinach, beans, peas, beets, onions, carrots, and turnips.

Cultivated fields range in size from 1000 to 3000 square feet, and tend to be located in or near the village, but not higher than about 5500 feet. The slopes directly below the village leading down to the Lonza and those above and to both sides of the village are dotted with potato or rye patches, again nearer the village because of the quality of land and the intensity of labor upon it.

43

Hay fields tend to be much larger than either gardens or cultivated fields, occasionally as large as an acre or more. They are found everywhere—high up on the sunny slope, below the forest on the shady side and, where there is unused space, even within the confines of the village. The only difference between grazing land and hay fields is the amount and quality of grass they produce, and this is by no means a precise division, but is a continuum that varies from year to year. If conditions are favorable a field may be harvested, but if the next year brings a late snow or too little sunshine, it may only be grazed. The distinction is made for tax purposes in the village land records, and is less specific in the minds of the villagers.

It is important to point out the role of various agricultural buildings located outside the village but below the alpine pastures. There are three types, each serving a different function in the agricultural cycle. The *Färich* is a stall situated high on the sunny slope, which is used in the fall to keep cattle or smaller animals while they are grazing on nearby fields. For this reason it is also called a *Weidestall*, or grazing land stall, for the animals are kept there but are not fed (Bachmann 1970:362). The second type is also unique to the slopes above the village. The *Zugscheune* is a temporary storage building where hay is kept after it has been harvested on nearby fields. The hay is cut during the summer, and is stored in this type of building until winter, when it can be transported to the village more easily by sled. The *Zugscheune* was also necessary when agriculture was at its peak, since there was not enough storage room in the village barns for all the hay required to feed the animals.

The final type of agricultural building on the slopes is the combination stall and hay barn, similar to that found in the village. The barn is used to store hay cut on nearby fields, much the same as the *Zugscheune*, except that there is a stall attached for keeping the animals who feed on the hay. Thus by bringing the animals up to the stall, the owner avoids having to transport the hay to the village, and at the same time he can collect manure to fertilize his fields the following spring. However, such buildings leave a definite impression on the pattern of life in the village. Since stall feeding occurs only during the winter months, the owner or a member of his family must walk up from the village daily to feed and milk the cows and clean out the stall, a task which requires a great amount of time and effort spent in unproductive transit. It is also the one task which seems to have been directly responsible for the majority of lives lost in avalanches, since it requires that people trek through the snow every day during the winter. (See Bloetzer 1964:204ff for a discussion of avalanche-related deaths throughout the history of the Lötschental.)

Factors affecting land use have been touched upon, but should be amplified to present a full picture of the problems of mountain agriculture. One of the most variable aspects is sunshine. Due to the direction of the valley, the villages are shielded from the morning sunlight by the mountain peaks on the south wall, so that during the winter Kippel receives barely three hours of sun, and on the longest day of summer only about 13 hours. The other villages of the valley are comparable in this respect. On the other hand, the sunny northern slope receives two to three hours more every day, which partially balances the difference in temperature resulting from the higher altitude. Across the valley, the southern slope is shut off from much of the sunshine that reaches the village, with the result that winter snow stays on the ground much longer, and even in the summer there can be an avalanche from unmelted snow high up on the slope.

Another danger is night frost, particularly damaging to gardens. It severely limits the vegetables that can be planted, and at the same time discourages experimentation. To a lesser extent it also affects the potato harvest and restricts the planting of grain to certain types that can survive under such conditions. Erosion is also a problem, whether caused by avalanche or simply the steep slopes of the valley. Whereas avalanches can be viewed as beneficial in the sense that they deposit soil at lower levels where it can be put to better use, this type of "beneficial erosion" creates difficulties at the same time, for it deposits a tremendous amount of unusable debris, mostly large rocks, which take up valuable space. Normal erosion on the slopes has been countered in many ways: in the Lötschental children were often assigned the task of carting soil from the bottom to the top of a parcel every spring.

As noted above, Valais is the driest canton in Switzerland. Throughout Valais, irrigation grew out of overpopulation, which in turn led to the need to expand the entire agricultural economy. As landholdings increased they moved away from natural sources of water, and complex systems of irrigation canals had to be constructed (Niederer 1956:22). Although the level of precipitation in the Lötschental is above the cantonal average, dryness is still a problem affecting agriculture, and to combat it valley residents have constructed an irrigation system, albeit one of relatively less complexity and importance than elsewhere in Valais.

One of the areas where the limitations imposed by the environment of the Lötschental are felt most heavily is that of the transportation and movement of goods and people. Until 1913 the only access to the valley was either over the Lötschen Pass from Kandersteg and the Bernese Highland, or up the steep, narrow gorge from Gampel and the Rhone Valley, and both of these routes were closed during much of the year due to deep snow and avalanche danger. Since 1922 there has been a wagon road from Goppenstein to Kippel, but not until after World War II was a paved road built extending from the train station into the back of the valley. Therefore the prewar agro-pastoral economy made no use of machinery, relying entirely upon human and animal energy to perform the necessary labor.

Transportation of food and other items from the outside was primarily by mule along the path from Gampel up the gorge into the inhabited area of the Lötschental. Wine, sugar, coffee, and additional grain were brought in from the Rhone Valley in this manner, and likewise the mail was hauled from the railroad station at Goppenstein into the valley after 1913. Mules were also occasionally used to carry humans, but usually only tourists with luggage, and animals never served as a regular means of transit within the valley. Horses were even less useful than mules because of the terrain.

The villagers were sometimes able to use the environment to their advantage by relying upon sleds for winter transport, but this could only be done in one

The sled offers the best means of transportation in winter. (Photo by Albert Nyfeler, courtesy of Professor Arnold Niederer)

direction—downward—and it was counteracted to some extent by the increased difficulty of upward movement in the snow. Thus the men would generally do as much of the work as possible during the summer, when they could climb the slopes more easily, and then wait until winter to transport the product (hay, wood, or whatever) down to the village where it would be used. But they were never free of the problems of upward transportation. Some of the hay could be brought down from the high pastures during the winter, but not all, for otherwise the manure would have to be carried up in the spring. Hauling manure from a high stall to a high field is a relatively easy task, but bringing it up from the village to the high fields and pastures, a difference in altitude of up to 2500 feet, would be prohibitively time consuming. It was easier, and more time was available, to take the cattle to the high stalls in the winter and make the daily trip to care for them, even though this entailed several hours in transit for a mere hour or so of work.

A network of roads along the slopes as well as on the valley floor would have solved this problem of vertical movement, but such a project was beyond the technology of the valley, not to mention the expense. The output of the economy would not have been increased by a factor sufficient to balance the cost, and so until recently a few paths to the alps were all that existed.

While the difficulty of transit and transportation in itself is evident, it is important to note how it fits into and in a sense molds the economy and life style of the valley. Vertical movement is frequently the single most important factor in planning and executing many tasks in the agro-pastoral economic system of the Lötschental and other alpine valleys. Transportation and transit affect land use, the annual cycle, patterns of cooperative labor, location and use of buildings—in short, movement is a fundamental consideration in the evolution of the valley, and we can expect it will continue to be so.

ALPS

The European mountain chain known as the Alps takes its name from its most prominent ecological and economic feature—the high pastures that ring each valley between the upper level of the forest and the glacier. Richard Weiss defines an alp as:

> . . . a grazing area in a mountainous region that lies at the upper limit of the productive zone, and contains the necessary huts and stalls; it is occupied for approximately three months during the summer by a herd of cattle, horses, or smaller animals (sheep, goats, or swine) under the direction of personnel chosen for that task, and serves as the chief place of residence and feeding for the animals. Alps with dairy animals, especially milk cows, are also characterized by a dairy operation with the appropriate personnel, buildings, and equipment (1941:53).

An alp thus has three basic attributes: it is in the mountains, usually above the existing domiciles; it contains various buildings; and it serves exclusively or

Hauling wood was formerly a community effort. (Photo by Albert Nyfeler, courtesy of Professor Arnold Niederer)

for the most part as a summer pasture, usually inhabited only during the summer pasture period and abandoned in the winter. The term "alp" is used to describe only those pastures in the Alps, but clearly similar situations can be found in the Jura, Caucasus, and Carpathian Mountains, as well as in Norway and other European mountain regions.

The alpine pasture is the highest productive land, and consequently is used exclusively for grazing due to its barrenness. High altitude hinders agriculture, for good cultivation is usually not possible above 5000 feet, a level that excludes 77.2 percent of the canton of Valais and 85.6 percent of the Lötschental. However, pasturage is possible up to about 8000 feet, depending upon the effects of glaciers and wind and snow conditions from year to year.

There are twelve alps in the Lötschental; seven are situated on the sunny side above the four villages, three are at the back of the valley behind Blatten, and two are on the shady side above the timber line at about 6500 feet. The latter two, Gattenalp and Nestalp, are more barren than the others and consequently are used mainly for sheep, as is Guggialp at the end of the valley. The actual pasturage rises as much as 2000 feet above the small group of huts that bears the name of the alp. The settlements themselves are located on a plateau running along the entire perimeter of the valley, but the pasturage is generally rocky and

Restialp, surrounded by steep and rocky pasture.

Faldumalp, located on a ridge safe from avalanche.

barren, its steep terrain covered with weeds and alpine flowers along with a sparse growth of grass.

Each settlement consists of a cluster of buildings called alp huts, built much like a house only smaller and with a stall taking the place of the cellar as the lower story. During the grazing period from late June through August, the alp hut performs four major functions—it serves as a stall for the cattle, sleeping quarters for the people who stay on the alp to tend the cattle, a work room with the equipment necessary for preparing dairy products, and a storage area for feed for the animals on days when the weather will not permit them to graze outdoors.

Like their counterparts in the villages, alp huts are inscribed both inside and out with poetic sayings, extolling the virtues of hard work and piety. Although most are similar to the inscriptions on houses, a few reveal a romantic feeling about the alp that is so much a part of the mountain person's life, indeed setting him off from his fellow countrymen in the lowlands or the city.

> Wenn's ein Eden gibt auf Erden,
> Kann's die Alpenhütte werden.
>
> If indeed there is an Eden upon earth,
> It could be the alp hut.

* * *

> Hoffnung schlummert tief im Herzen
> Wie im Lylienkelch der Thau.

Hoffnung thaucht wie aus den Wolken
Nach dem Sturm des Himmels Blau.

Hope slumbers deep in the heart,
As in a lily cup lies dew.
Hope appears, as after a storm
Out of the clouds shines heaven's blue.

Each alp settlement has its own chapel, usually a prominent building standing out from the cluster of huts surrounding it. Several of them also have a hôtel open during the summer, or at least a hut converted into a restaurant/tavern to serve the numerous summer tourists who wander about the high pastures or hike along the high mountain trails. The hotel on Fafleralp was built in 1908, and the *Gasthaus* on Kummenalp in 1928, with later lodgings added at Fafleralp in 1930, and on Faldumalp in 1936 and Lauchernalp in 1941 (Siegen 1959:38–40).

Ownership and management of the alp are important variables affecting the entire economic system of the valley. Ownership of the pasture may be in the hands of the corporation of burghers, the citizens of the community, as in the case of Blühenden and Nestalp, both of which belong to the commune of Blatten. The alp is then usually located within the boundaries of the community that owns it, but this is not always the case, as when a particular community has a shortage of pasturage and purchases or trades for an alp in another neighboring

Typical alp hut, with living quarters atop a stall.

Chapel at Hockenalp.

community. Each citizen, or burgher, has certain rights regarding the use of the alp and obligations concerning its maintenance.

In order to prevent the destruction of the grazing land through overpopulation, the number of animals must be restricted in some way. One method is to allow each burgher to graze only as many animals as he can keep and feed during the winter, using hay and other feed originating within the community and not purchased from outside. This system thus regulates use of the alp in direct relation to the size of a person's holdings (Niederer 1956:41). Another way of regulating use and protecting the alp is to assign it a certain value according to the number of cattle it can take without declining in quality. These rights are then divided among the burghers according to various patterns: (a) all burghers have equal rights regardless of whether they can support that number of animals over the winter or not. This is the case described by Imboden for Embd, in the nearby Vispertal, where each family has the right to graze two cows on the community-owned alp (1956:52); (b) Each person is given a varying number of grazing rights in proportion to the number of cattle he can feed over the winter, and relative to the total number of cattle wintered by all burghers. This is the case in the village of Bellwald, in the upper Rhone Valley region known as Goms (Schmid 1969:150); (c) Alp rights are divided according to the amount of hay a person produces and harvests; (d) Rights are divided and distributed according to the amount of hay-producing meadow a person owns;

(e) Rights are distributed according to the amount or value of all the land a person owns.

The second type of alp ownership and management is the *Genossenschaftsalp*, an association of private individuals, in theory independent of the community, who own and administer the grazing area. Membership restriction has the effect of protecting the alp, just as artificial restrictions are employed for the community-owned alp. How the alp is operated depends to some extent, but not entirely, upon how it is owned. The basic dichotomy is between a system of communal management and one in which each individual user maintains a separate stall and dairy operation.

In the Lötschental we generally find the undivided association-owned alp with individual labor. Each member with animals on the alp has his own hut and stall, cares for his own animals, and performs his own dairy labor. Buildings generally belong to the individuals and not the association. An exception is presented by Weritzalp, in the commune of Wiler. Here the alp is owned by a corporate association and it is operated by persons employed by the association, who are charged with the care of the entire herd and with the related dairy operation. Although each member has his own stall, the work is still done communally.

Many readily apparent factors point to the individual alpine operation as a highly irrational system. For one thing, there is the duplication of effort

The roof of a typical alp hut, held down by heavy rocks.

unnecessarily spent on herding the animals individually when they could as easily be herded together. And even where communal herding occurs, whether by rotation of owners or by personnel hired jointly by them, individual dairying is extremely wasteful, for one owner by himself has too much milk to drink and too little to make cheese from—top quality cheese is not possible without a large number of cattle to produce enough milk with high fat content. Then, too, this system is usually characterized by an "alp village," a group of huts much larger than that required by a communal-type system. Consequently the use of wood, not only for buildings but for firewood and even wooden tools and utensils, is much greater and more expensive (Leibundgut 1938:54).

In view of all these negative attributes, why does the individual dairy operation still exist? The reasons for its persistence, the impediments to its disappearance, are not readily apparent. Weiss notes the deep-rooted obstinacy of the mountain peasants, their refusal to allow strangers to care for their animals, and their romantic glorification of the time spent on the alp, promoting it to a "summer resort" for the old, the women, and the children (1941:87). Informants' responses in Kippel seem to bear out Weiss' notion of the basis for the retention of the individual management system in the Lötschental. One man claimed that it was healthier for the women and children to spend the summer on the alp. He also noted that it would be too expensive to have to pay the necessary herding and dairying personnel, ignoring however the expense of the extra buildings required, the extra time consumed, and the fact that a few decades ago the changeover to communal dairying could have been made without incurring the expense of today's cost of labor. Another reason might be because no outsiders own and use grazing rights to Lötschenthal alps, except the sheep alps, which are left untended anyway. This means that whereas in some valleys nonresident alp users would have to hire herders and dairy workers no matter what system were used, in the Lötschental all could be done by local residents. Another man stated that one reason was that the time spent on the alp was the "peasant's vacation" (*Ferien der Landwirte*), i.e. the best days of their lives. He also mentioned that the girls who used to work up on the alp and spend the entire summer there were very fond of this period in their lives, and if they had to stay in the village they would have gone elsewhere to find employment, a claim which incidentally is generally refuted by young girls who have spent the summer on the alp. Finally, Niederer suggests two further possible reasons for the retention of the individual operation. One, he claims, is the influence of courting patterns that are frequently highly specialized to cope with and overcome the separation of young boys and girls during the summer. He also notes that the inherent distrustfulness of the Valais peasant plays a role in his lack of willingness to allow another person to "interfere" in his economic life. This is a recurrent theme in popular sayings and stories throughout the canton of Valais, particularly the fear of having milk stolen or "underreported," that is, reported to be a lesser volume than was actually produced (Niederer: personal communication).

When all of these factors are combined—the location of the village, the ownership of the alp, the personality of the peasant, his courting patterns, and his romantic notions—we find that there is no single definitive answer to the question of why the individual alpine management system still exists. It is, indeed, as Weiss claims:

> . . . the difference between individual and communal dairy operations and their resultant distribution cannot be explained by one factor alone, but only by many different ecological, economic, and historical factors that have conditioned or fostered one system or the other (1941:95).

The alps are assessed according to the number of animals they can feed, a figure usually based on five acres of grazing land for each full grown milk cow. Once a total number of units has been assessed, the resulting use-rights are broken down into more applicable figures: thus a full grown milk-giving cow counts for one unit, or one "cow"; a cow approaching maturity but which has not yet borne a calf counts for "1/2 cow"; a calf counts for "1/4 cow"; and sheep and goats are equal to varying amounts to "1/10 cow." This system is frequently calculated in terms of "feet"—a cow equals four feet, a young cow two, a calf one, a goat one-half, etc.

Membership in an alp association is limited to those who hold a certain number of use-rights derived from this assessment, which they have acquired either through inheritance or purchase. In the case of Hockenalp in Kippel, the minimum for full voting membership is "1/2 cow." Along with the right to pasture animals and build a hut, stall, and cellar on the alp goes a series of duties and obligations designed to maintain and improve the quality of the pasture, to raise money to pay taxes levied by the community, and generally to preserve order and assure the smooth functioning of the association. Although membership is not restricted to residents of the Lötschental in the sense that a person does not forfeit his rights if he emigrates, and his descendants may inherit them even though they are not natives of the valley, nonetheless preventive measures have been taken to assure that the alps would not fall into the hands of outsiders with no ties to the Lötschental. An act recorded in the Kippel archives, dated 10 March 1497, declares that ". . . no one may sell or lease alp rights to outsiders, under penalty of confiscation," except when the outsider owns a certain amount of property within the valley, deemed sufficient to support the animals for the remainder of the year.

The alp association functions as follows: early in the summer the members hold their annual meeting, the *Alprechnung* (alp reckoning). There they determine how many animals each member will graze on the alp that summer; should that number be greater than the total number of alp rights a person owns, then he must lease sufficient unused rights from other members (if they are available) at a rate fixed by the association statutes. When this has been taken care of, the members decide upon the date for ascending to the alp, based upon previous weather conditions and the need to wait for the grass on the pastures to grow, balanced against the severity of the winter and the amount of hay members have left in the village. Once the cows are on the alp, the task of herding them is shared by all participating members. One owner is responsible for herding all the cattle each day, according to a system of rotation based on the number of cows each has on the alp. On Hockenalp this works out so that for every four cows a person has on the alp he must herd one day in the cycle or rotation (number of cows on alp ÷ 4 — number of days in cycle). Thus if a person has four cows on the alp out of a total of 96, he must herd one day in 24. If he has only three cows there, he must herd one day in 24 for the first three rotations, and then he is free for the fourth. The herder's responsibility lasts from morning, when the cattle are taken out to pasture, until evening when they are returned to their respective stalls. Thereupon each owner must milk his own cows, and in most cases prepare his own dairy products as well.

Maintenance, preparation, and improvement of the alp are carried out before and after its occupation during the summer. The most common tasks include carting and scattering manure, clearing the land of avalanche debris, repairing roads, bridges, fountains, and fences. Each member must work (or provide a worker) one day for each cow he has on the alp that particular year. Since the work is divided between spring and fall, those with more cattle work both seasons, those with fewer work only one. There are also special occasions requiring extra work, and this is then apportioned along the same lines, according to the number of cattle each person has on the alp relative to the total.

Before going on, we should consider the role of the alp in the agro-pastoral economy of the mountain region in general, particularly as compared to other pastoral economic systems found in Europe. Clearly the alp cannot be considered an economic whole, for it must be used in conjunction with other areas of the valley in order to support an agro-pastoral economy. The alp merely supplies the summer food for the animals, while the valley provides for the other three seasons. The use of the alp in this manner requires a certain amount of movement within the valley.

In conclusion, what can be said about the performance of the typical alpine economic system? It is interesting to note that two men quite familiar with the economic problems of the Alps take opposing views, based on a different emphasis. Loup describes it as a rational economic activity, particularly the communal exploitation of the alpine pastures, for it requires few people to operate and it is highly organized (1965:242). On the other hand, Bellwald claims that because of the great differences in altitude which can lead to as much as 60 percent of the human labor being spent in transit, the alpine economy is highly irrational (1963:34).

It is perhaps most instructive to view the economic activities of the mountain peasants in terms of the alternatives open to them. If they reject other possibilities which would yield a greater income for the time spent on agriculture and at the same time would not reduce their standard of living by depriving them of the side benefits of their agricultural operation, then we can consider it irrational for them to continue as agro-pastoralists. In other words, is their retention of their traditional economic activity a sentimental choice or a calculated decision based upon their evaluation of the opportunities open to them? This question will be discussed in subsequent chapters, and it will become clear in the conclusion that whereas the "opportunity cost" of agro-pastoralism relative to other possible sources of income was low in the prewar era, it has become increasingly higher since 1945.

OWNERSHIP

Three distinct types of ownership exist in Kippel: the alp associations own and operate the high pastures; the community, both in a political and a religious sense, owns land and buildings of all types; and the individual households each have their own private holdings. I have already discussed the functions of the alp association and turn here to the community and the individual.

The community has acquired or retained possession of various goods, primarily land and buildings. Before the replacement of the subsistence economy with a cash economy, the community's main concern was to supply itself with the necessities for communal affairs through the yield of the land it owned. One such need was the maintenance of the communally owned breeding bull, which entailed working and harvesting hay fields. Thus there had to be a stall for the bull and enough barns to store the hay. Village festivals likewise required various products supplied through communal labor.

• Not surprisingly, some of the choicest hay and grain fields and the largest and sturdiest buildings belong to the community. Included in this public property is most of the forest land, which supplies the villagers with avalanche protection and with wood for heating, cooking, and construction. The sawmill is community owned as is the now defunct baking oven. Finally, various buildings with a primarily communal purpose are also village property, notably the schoolhouse and the village hall.

The church is in a similar position to the community in that it must provide for certain aspects of its own maintenance, and in the prewar days this meant working its own land. The clergymen earlier were supported by the yield from church-owned land. The holdings of the church also helped support members who were poverty stricken and needed the assistance of the community, although here the distinction between the church community and the municipal community becomes blurred, for ultimately it is the corporation of burghers that holds the legal responsibility for assisting a needy member.

Church and communal land holdings are scattered and fragmented, and the buildings are likewise scattered to conform more or less to these holdings. To understand this we must turn to private ownership. One of the clearest examples of how the alpine ecosystem affects the annual cycle is the staggered hay harvest, which begins on the bottom of the sunny side and moves up to the lower edge of the alp, then returns to the lower shady side, and finally moves back across the valley floor once again. But even within the same general area there can be tremendous variation. A spot may be favored in terms of sunshine, lack of proximity to an avalanche lane, the location of an irrigation canal, rate of erosion—these and other factors disallow any generalization about even the most limited section of the valley. A potato patch might be just a few feet away from a rockpile, or perhaps the peak of a hill separates beautiful hay meadows from barren, eroded, avalanche-torn grazing land.

Prior to the war, the main goal of the mixed agricultural economy was subsistence. Despite the shortage of a few essential items, notably wine, sugar, salt, and coffee, as well as supplementary grain supplies, the basic orientation remained toward production for consumption. Ideally each agricultural operation, be it an individual, a household, or a group of households, was self-sufficient, and to be so each unit had to use a variety of land and buildings. In terms of ownership, this meant that if the valley were to support a large population on a limited amount of resources, there could be no large, continuous estates that would monopolize one type of land. Each household needed grazing land in addition to the alpine pastures to use before and after the term on the alp; each needed hay fields that yielded enough hay to feed the animals through the winter; and of course there were the needs of the family, requiring potato and grain fields as well as a garden. In addition, each agricultural operation had to have a variety of buildings—stalls to keep the animals during the winter, hay barns, granaries, and storage sheds for various household products.

All these economic demands point to a definite vertical emphasis concerning land use within the valley. For not only does a person need enough hay fields to feed his animals, he needs some close to the village that he can harvest in July and again in September, and he needs others higher up that he can harvest in August. More important, *everyone* needs hay fields that they can harvest according to the limitations imposed by the staggered harvest season. Not only does a person need enough potato and grain fields to feed his family, but they must be dispersed so that in a bad year, a rainy year, a year of many avalanches, a year of floods, he will still have enough to survive. And again, by extension, this is true for every household. The result of the demands upon the land by the valley economy, and by each individual economic unit, is the fragmentation of land. The system of individual proprietorship can only exist and support the entire population of the valley when land is fragmented so that each individual operation has the necessary varied prerequisites for subsistence.

The agricultural census of 1939 describes the extent of fragmentation. The typical agricultural holding of about nine acres is divided into an average of 51 parcels, scattered throughout the village and most likely even into the neighboring communes of Ferden and Wiler. In addition, plots of land generally range in altitude from about 4500 feet on the valley floor to 6500 feet at the foot of the alps.

Fragmentation has both positive and negative effects upon life in the Lötschental. Aside from its obvious necessity in the agricultural sphere, allowing for the variety of land and dispersion of buildings required by the valley economy, the division of land into many parcels protects the individual owner from a localized disaster. At the same time, fragmentation enables the farmer to spread out his peak work periods, such as planting and harvesting, due to the variation in altitude and exposure of different parcels of land. But most important, the fact that there are no large, continuous estates means that everyone has a chance at subsistence—all types of land at all levels are thus available to each individual.

On the other hand, fragmentation has its negative aspects as well. The dispersion of plots requires an inordinate expenditure of time on transportation and transit. One woman told of an experience in the early days of her marriage when she spent the summer tending her family's cattle on Faldumalp, above the village of Ferden. In the late summer she had to harvest a number of hay fields, and on one particular day she had to walk to a field just below Weritzalp, some two and a half hours away, to cut the hay there. When she finished, she walked back to Faldumalp to milk and feed her cattle, only to return to the field the next day to rake up the dried hay and carry it to a nearby barn. This example, where a woman is required to spend over ten hours walking from her summer residence to a single hay field just to perform a few hours work harvesting hay, illustrates the role of transit time in the total allocation of time and labor in the agricultural economy. Altitude becomes an overpowering factor—thus it was easier for her to go to the field from the alp at about the same altitude than for her husband to go from Kippel, which, although much closer in space, was indeed much farther in time because of the ascent of some 2000 feet.

A second disadvantage of fragmentation is the fact that it inhibits the use of machinery, even something as simple as the plow. Clearly it is uneconomical to use a large machine on a small plot, not to mention the lack of service roads.

Cultivated fields near the village. Each plot belongs to a different owner.

Yet if there were a road to each parcel, there would be more road surface than fields! Finally there is the problem of the shape of fields—fragmentation, coupled with the terrain, leads to the formation of irregular shaped parcels which defy rational management. Many a relatively large parcel is unsuited for a building because it is long and narrow, or because it curves around a tree or a ridge.

Not all land is fragmented to the same degree. Gardens, located within the limited confines of the village, tend to be the smallest parcels. Moreover, the land in and near the village tends to be the most expensive, which limits the size of gardens even further. The yield from a small plot is generally sufficient for the needs of most households during the summer, and in winter the diet is supplemented when possible with the purchase of imported fruits and vegetables. Finally, in dividing an estate for inheritance, land in the village takes on added value as a possible building site, and therefore garden plots tend to be divided more than other types of land because they are more desirable in this sense. Cultivated fields in and near the village are the next most limited type of land, due to the effects of altitude upon the crops grown. Not surprisingly, then, they are next to gardens the most fragmented type of land. The law of supply and demand obviously has a direct effect upon the rate of fragmentation.

A consequence of the division of land into numerous small parcels is the dispersion and profusion of buildings. Since the yield from a normal sized hay field will not come near filling a barn, the alternatives are to build smaller barns, to transport the hay over greater distances, or to build and use them jointly. Transportation in the summer is time consuming and tedious, and especially undesirable at the peak of the agricultural labor cycle. To build a barn only large enough to store the hay from one field would be wasteful and expensive in terms of both labor and material. The best solution, it would seem, is to join together with others who own nearby fields and build a barn large enough for the yield from many parcels.

Of all the different types of buildings the *Stadel*, or granary, tends to be divided among the most co-owners. This is primarily because the major investment in the granary is the threshing floor, while the amount of space needed to store the grain before it is threshed is relatively small, and can be supplemented by another type of storage building. The *Speicher*, or general storage shed, has fewer divisions due to the nature of the goods usually kept in it, since division entails the construction of an interior partition and the addition of a door on the outside wall.

Given the situation with the land, the joint ownership of buildings is essentially beneficial. The large number of scattered agricultural buildings enables more intensive use of the land by providing necessary space and equipment on or near the actual site of the labor. The dispersion of stalls leads to a more widespread use of manure, which in turn increases the yield from the fields. Joint construction and maintenance saves time and valuable resources. In the long run, the divided ownership of buildings is efficient in many ways, for despite the enormous expenditure of time in transit, were it not for nearby buildings, that time would be more than doubled in transporting products to and from the village.

INHERITANCE

Fragmentation, grounded in the idea of a subsistence economy, is perpetuated and regulated to a certain extent through customs and laws, such as the division of inheritance, public ownership of land, and communal labor upon it. Public ownership serves as a supplement to the individual operation, providing both additional resources, such as grazing land, and restricted or limited resources, such as wood. Communal labor enables the weak as well as the strong to benefit from the combined assets of all. Inheritance provides for the division of the estate into equal portions, so that each heir has at least a minimal amount of each of the prerequisites necessary to begin an individual operation at the minimal subsistence level.

The pattern found in the Lötschental and throughout the mountain cantons of Switzerland is a classic example of partible inheritance, whereby each heir, regardless of age or sex, receives an equal part of the estate. Although Swiss federal law states that an agricultural operation must be inherited intact if one of the male heirs who is capable of managing it requests it, in the cantons where the tradition of partible inheritance is strong (i.e. Valais, Grisons, and Ticino), the judge has the option of denying such a request, if he finds it in the interest of the other heirs to do so. In Valais for all practical purposes impartible inheritance does not exist, for the custom of equal division among all heirs is so strong.* Under partible inheritance as it is practiced in the Lötschental, theoretically every single item in the estate is subject to division, although this is never the case. Generally the subdivision of parcels of land or portions of buildings only occurs when it is necessary to balance the lots of each of the heirs, or when the value of a particular item is disputed.

The primary goal in dividing up an estate for inheritance is that each heir receives property of all kinds, at various levels and destined for various uses. This is considered necessary as the basis of a viable agricultural operation. Thus each lot must contain a garden and some arable land near the village and a number of hay fields and meadows scattered about the slopes. Agricultural buildings are also dispensed with an eye toward the division of land, so that they can be used in conjunction with nearby parcels. A functional unit, called a *Heiwlin*, has in fact evolved based upon the relationship between buildings and land; this term describes a series of meadows in proximity to a building of which at least part belongs to the owner of the meadows (Bachmann 1970:212). Another factor that sometimes enters into consideration when dividing an estate is the present or anticipated residence of various members of the family. If a daughter, for example, is married or engaged to a man from Wiler, and the estate includes property there, she would most likely receive it as part or all of her share of the inheritance.

The major exception to the joint use and inheritance of buildings is the house, or even a flat within a house. When a multiunit house is built, it is usually the joint project of brothers or close relatives. They customarily wait until after the

---

* I am indebted to Professor Arnold Niederer for pointing out this technicality to me.

work is complete to decide which unit belongs to whom. In this way they can insure equal cooperation on the entire project, for if they knew beforehand which flat was which, the work might not be equal on both. This strict emphasis on equality among siblings in building a house parallels the inheritance practice in some cases, where instead of calling in a disinterested third party to divide the estate, the task is assigned to one of the heirs. That person then divides the estate into the proper number of lots, with the stipulation that the others choose theirs first and he gets the one that remains. Thus in order to make sure he receives an equal share he must divide the estate as evenly as possible.

In some cases a division cannot be made in spatial terms, and so a temporal one is made instead. This practice is found primarily in the case of stalls, which due to their interior structure cannot be divided beyond the number of separate cubicles they contain. Thus the rights to a stall might be distributed according to a time schedule, with each owner using it for part of the year according to his fractional holding in it. This is particularly effective if the ownership of the stall is paralleled by ownership in an attached barn. In such a case a man who owned a quarter of the stall and sufficient space in the barn, along with one or more nearby hay fields, would thus possess a complete functional unit—he could grow, harvest, and store the hay and then feed it to his cattle all within one small area.

An exception to exact division sometimes occurs with alp rights. It is important to maintain a minimum portion of an alp right (for Hockenalp it is "1/2 cow"). The right to vote on the affairs of the association, the right to build a hut, and to receive remuneration for unused rights, all are based on a certain minimal holding. To divide the alp rights of an estate beyond this minimal holding would be a self-defeating proposition, and therefore in most cases such a division is avoided by compensating some heirs with other kinds of property from the estate if necessary.

In a few cases the estate is not divided among the heirs, but instead an alternative action is taken by forming an "association of heirs," or *Erbgemeinschaft*. No division whatsoever takes place, and the estate remains the common property of all the heirs, either to be worked as a single unit or separately according to the agreement that is reached. The *Erbgemeinschaft* is found especially where the heirs form a common household, as in the case of a number of unmarried siblings. If subsequent to the joint inheritance one member should decide to split off and start his or her own family, a share may be allocated informally or else a separate formal division may be made. More likely, however, the new spouse will bring new land into the joint holding and simply work along with the common labor force, although new residential patterns will emerge.

An *Erbgemeinschaft* was sometimes formed out of poverty, if the estate were so small that any division would render it incapable of supporting a household. With an extremely limited amount of a particular type of land, division might leave each heir's share of that type useless. Of course, once such a joint household was formed it became very difficult to break up. If one or more members took their shares out of the total holding, those remaining would suffer. This led to extreme internal pressure in favor of celibacy—except in the case where a member could marry someone willing to join in the common economic arrangement and contribute his or her inheritance to the total holding.

At other times an *Erbgemeinschaft* might be formed out of wealth, as an effort on the part of the parents to preserve the estate for future generations. Inheritance practices dictate that if a person dies childless, the estate is divided among the siblings or their descendants, and does not go to the surviving spouse, should there be one. Thus if a wealthy man with many children could prevent all but one or two from marrying, then ultimately the entire estate would fall back into the hands of the one or two married descendants and their families, for as the single siblings died their share would ultimately revert to their nieces and nephews. In such a case the unmarried siblings would form a joint household, while the married heirs would reside separately, but have use rights to a larger portion of the estate.

An individual's holding before marriage is rarely enough to support a family, and this is one reason for the high rate of endogamy. It stands to reason that if a boy marries a girl from the Lötschental he will have twice as much land to work as if he marries a girl from outside the valley. In addition there are a number of different ways of putting together enough land to make a viable agricultural holding: (a) by adding land belonging to relatives who are taken into the household for that express purpose; (b) single siblings in a combined household pooling their inheritance (i.e. the *Erbgemeinschaft* described above); (c) the total holdings of an undivided *Erbgemeinschaft*, but not necessarily from one single household; (d) renting unused land to supplement one's own.

Even in the tight years during the Depression, when the population was high and land was scarce, renting was a common means of increasing agricultural output. The fee was generally a percentage of the yield, although in more recent years a cash payment has been substituted. Since good agricultural land was always at a premium, leasing it to someone else was not particularly desirable as a source of income for the owner, but frequently an unbalanced holding dictated this as the only course. That is, a man might have more hay fields than his household could harvest in one summer, while at the same time he might be lacking a field suitable for grain or potatoes. Moreover, in rare cases land owned by the church would be let out to private citizens, either to raise money to cover expenses or else to serve as a more dignified means of assisting the poorer members of the community. A person who rented land always owned property, but the right combination of all kinds of land and buildings, or enough of a particular kind, was not always possible.

COOPERATIVE LABOR

Life in the Alps is based upon a series of unique adaptations enabling a population to overcome the harsh environment. Many of these features have been described in the preceding pages: the clustered villages safe from avalanche; the scattered agricultural buildings and fragmented holdings affording a variety of land use where a shortage of usable land exists; a system of partible inheritance to maintain the relative equality, or at least the equal opportunity necessary for the protection of future generations.* These adaptations are the result of increasing population pressures upon limited resources. With only a few farmsteads in the valley, extreme solutions would not be necessary, but if the valley is to support a high population density, adaptations such as a high degree of land specialization must come about. The success of these adaptations is predicated above all upon communal or cooperative labor (*Gemeinwerk*), since an individual or even an entire household is frequently unable to surmount the difficulties imposed by the steep terrain, the raw and forbidding climate, or the short and compact agricultural season.

Communal labor is but a small part of the cooperative system which exists within the village, extending to all aspects of village life—interest groups, associations centered around various resources within the community, even religious and secular celebrations. In addition a wide range of cooperation exists in the Lötschental, from simple reciprocation among individuals or families to situations in which the entire community joins together to carry out a particular task. In this sense, mutual aid can be seen as an extension of the principle of joint ownership and use of property. For example, the scarcity of work animals, due to high overhead costs and low output, often led to joint ownership and use of mules. From there it is but a short step to the situation whereby the owner lends his mule to a needy neighbor, perhaps to transport heavy equipment up to the alp or to bring a load of wood into the village, and in return the neighbor sends his son to help with the owner's hay harvest. For more difficult tasks, several men might get together to help each other out, thereby saving time over each doing his own job alone. Plowing or hoeing fields in the spring or harvesting hay in the fall are examples of such work, where cooperation is more effective than individual effort. In some cases an arrangement is reached whereby each contributes something different according to his means, so that one man might supply the mule, another the necessary tools, and a third the majority of the labor. Such favors or instances of cooperation are generally reciprocated on a day-to-day or job-to-job basis so that a relative balance is maintained, but the potential of help in times of need is important enough that an exact balance need not be struck and closely adhered to.

Another occasion for communal labor is the moving of cattle from stall to stall during the winter. Depending upon the distance and the snow conditions, the owner may call upon just a few men from the village, or he might require the entire male population. If only a few men are needed, they can either be chosen by lot or else the man can ask his closest friends to volunteer. The success of this system is based upon reciprocation, and although there are no legal sanctions requiring a person to repay his labor debt, social pressure is always enough, for the threat of withholding aid is indeed a threat of economic ruin and social isolation.

---

* Partible inheritance is not the only form found in the Alps. Impartible inheritance can be equally effective as a social mechanism to conquer the environmental hazards of alpine agriculture (see Cole 1969).

Shearing the sheep, another cooperative effort. (Photo by Albert Nyfeler, courtesy of Professor Arnold Niederer)

This type of temporary *ad hoc* mutual assistance among a few individuals should be distinguished from the more enduring associations. Formal corporations such as the alp or the dairy cooperative have a restrictive membership based upon entrance either through purchase or inheritance of use-rights. There is a written code of procedure that governs the activities of the association as a whole and of its members as individuals under certain circumstances. Each member is required to invest a certain amount of labor in the maintenance of the property of the association, and in the performance of duties for the benefit of the member-ship as a whole. We have already seen how this works in the alp association, where each member is required to put in a specified amount of time on com-munal labor for the maintenance and improvement of the alp, and further labor in taking his turn watching over the entire herd of cattle during the summer grazing period. Less formal are the irrigation associations, one for each canal. Although in some cases there are written documents regulating the use of the canals, more often common understanding prevails. Membership is restricted only in the sense that to be a member a person must own land adjacent to the canal, but this is a different basis than that of a formal association. A person is a member by virtue of the location of his land holding, and not by virtue of his (or his ancestor's) intent to join. Hence it is not a voluntary association.

The most impressive, if not the most important form of cooperative labor, is that in which the entire community takes part. There are two variants of this type: labor for the individual, that is for the direct benefit of one or more specific individuals at one time, and labor for the entire community, in which case the personal gain may be either direct or indirect. Any individual may call upon his community to come to his aid for a variety of reasons. A common example occurs when a man wishes to build an alp hut. While building the hut is the owner's responsibility, transporting the wood to the alp is beyond his means. Thus the prospective builder can request that the entire male population of his village between the ages of fifteen and sixty (the *Mannstand*) assist him in carrying the wood. For this service he must pay a nominal fee to the village treasury and supply wine for all the workers. If a villager cannot be present he must provide a replacement from another village at his own cost. However, from all accounts of the festivities accompanying this task, absenteeism was not a problem.

Another example of communal labor for the direct benefit of individuals is

Moving cattle through deep snow requires a solid path.

Sawing beams for construction. (Photo by Albert Nyfeler, courtesy of Professor Arnold Niederer)

the hay transport in winter, actually made over into a festival in the neighboring village of Wiler. The task of bringing hay down to the village from the scattered *Zugscheunen* or hay barns is really an individual one, but the manner in which it is carried out gives it a communal air. The dangers and difficulties of transporting large burdens in the snow are such that there is a certain safety in numbers, and like the wood transport, it becomes an important festive occasion in the social life of the village.

Mutual aid frequently occurs when illness or death renders a family unable to perform the necessary work to maintain itself. Relatives and other villagers pitch in to assist the family through the crisis. In fact, in many cases the priest even allows such labor to be performed on Sundays, so that those who help out need not sacrifice their own production, a particularly important consideration around harvest time (Niederer 1956:69).

General communal labor for the benefit of all, either for the municipal community or the church, is perhaps the purest form of cooperative labor, since the yield from the communal fields goes for the festive occasions involving the entire community. Other communal projects deal with tasks such as avalanche protection, road building and maintenance, and flood control. Nonetheless, natural catastrophes cannot be prevented, and when one does occur mutual assistance comes to the fore. In 1900, for example, when the entire village of Wiler burned to the ground, Kippel, the nearest neighboring village, took in the residents of Wiler while they rebuilt their homes.

Kinship ties create channels of cooperation for tasks too large for one household, but not of such magnitude as to require the entire community. Construction of a house or other building is usually carried out by brothers or brothers-in-law. A man who needs help hauling a heavy load will go first to a relative for aid. Someone seeking a reciprocal arrangement by which he can obtain a product or service he lacks will seek out a relative with a complementary need. A newly acquired son-in-law will share the agricultural duties with his father-in-law and any other members of the latter's household still around. Even in renting land or buildings, kinship is a factor in the ultimate choice.

In postwar times, when more men have found employment outside the valley, yet commute to work and maintain an agricultural operation as well, the kinship network has become even more important. Now not only the wife of the worker, but perhaps his sisters or even sisters-in-law will share in the agro-pastoral duties, and ultimately in the yield. Providing enough hay to feed two sheep for the winter might earn a woman and her family one of those sheep for their own use. Whereas before the war the kinship network supplied extra labor on specific occasions when it was needed, the more the men leave the village, the more the women must rely upon increased labor from that network to keep the agricultural operation going.

In some cases cooperation among several households can encompass the entire agricultural sphere, and not merely isolated tasks. This might be the result either of an exceptional *Erbgemeinschaft* which has been maintained after several siblings have married, pooling the inheritance of the newly-acquired in-laws as well, or it might only be a question of insufficient holdings to provide subsistence for all if divided. The division of labor is likely to be more clear-cut in such a situation, due to the larger labor force. One group in Kippel stands out as an example of cooperation within an extended family acting as a single economic unit. After the premature death of their father, eight surviving children and their mother developed a strong bond that has kept the siblings together throughout their lives. Economic pressures were not so great that they were forced to remain in a single household, perhaps because the two eldest boys and later the youngest as well had cash incomes, the eldest in a factory and the other two as members of the Papal Guard. As a result, four of the eight siblings (all girls) married, moving into their husbands' households. A fifth girl remained single and stayed in the household of the three males. Despite the absence of four siblings, the inheritance was never divided. The holdings of the four brothers-in-law were added (practically, not legally) to the total and are still worked together. The entire operation is adapted to the individuals involved, so that some males work at other jobs, and some solely in agriculture. The yield of the agro-pastoral efforts is divided according to a formula set up by the members of this extended family group, so that both input and output are regulated by the needs and particular situations of each. The primary product is, of course, milk, which each member household receives for its efforts toward the maintenance and support of the operation. Although for the most part only two or three men work full time at agriculture, the women are always around to help, and when a major task comes along, such as at harvest time, the entire family, including dozens of helpers, can be seen working in the fields together.

This is admittedly an extreme case, but it is not out of the ordinary to find numerous networks among related nuclear families. Older people who cannot cope with the labor necessary to maintain animals are happy to have someone work their land for them in return for milk and occasional other products, while younger men who lack enough land are glad to make such a reciprocal agreement. If arrangements are made within the same generation, the relationship tends to be rather close, perhaps siblings or in-laws. If, on the other hand, such an arrangement spans two generations, it might be further apart, for a parent-child relationship would generally occur within the same household, although more recently with the decline of the extended family and a strong tendency toward neolocal residence as a prerequisite for marriage this pattern has changed. Today in Kippel there are 32 households involved in some sort of cooperative effort in the agricultural sphere, and in every case the households in each group are tied together by bonds of kinship. The rest of the households either manage their agriculture alone, or else have given it up completely. In most cases, however, there is little left to manage, for the main agricultural families are almost all involved in a cooperative arrangement.

It is reasonable to assume that in the prewar era the situation regarding cooperation on this level was similar to what it is today, in that households were tied together by a bond primarily arising out of kinship. Of course, many more families lived from agriculture, and a larger proportion of each family was involved in the agro-pastoral operation, which in turn meant that the role of cooperation was different than it is today. Yet the forces of poverty within the valley meant that relatively more labor had to be put into agriculture, and more labor demanded more cooperation. There is no evidence to suggest that the ties that bind families together today in small-scale cooperative ventures were not present earlier.

SOCIAL INTERACTION

Voluntary associations form another network of relationships among the villagers, separate from kinship ties. Kämpfen suggests that the history of associations within alpine villages is closely related to the situation of corporate village life (1942:20). He discusses primarily economic based associations, such as those dealing with the use of pasture, water, or communal land, which he says are directly caused by the need to join together to overcome the elements. Clearly the ecological demands upon mountain dwellers were met largely through the combined efforts of many people in a way that could not be equalled by each individual working separately in his own interest. We might therefore question whether such associations were in fact voluntary, for no real choice could be made. One participated in various associations because it was the only way one could survive.

It is not surprising that out of this tradition of mutual aid and close contact, not only among kinsmen but among all residents of any community, a network of extra-kin social relationships should develop to reinforce the ties of kinship already binding the villagers to one another. In Kippel, as in most alpine villages, this network is manifested in a large number of voluntary associations dealing with various aspects of the social life within the village. Over a dozen groups cover a wide range of interests, from music and sports to religious duties and occupational activities.

In the realm of music and entertainment there are four separate groups. The village band has about 25 members. Formed in 1890, it has provided music for festive occasions as well as religious ceremonies of all kinds. The members rehearse regularly, give concerts periodically to raise money to meet their expenses, and represent the village at music festivals and even in competitions throughout the canton. The church choir is another music group with a separate but not mutually exclusive membership. Its primary function is to sing at high mass and other church ceremonies of major importance, but secular performances and concerts are also given. A third music group is new in 1970, and includes members from all four villages in the Lötschental. It is a junior brass band, organized for the young boys of the valley in an attempt to maintain interest in music. Its primary function is to offer the youngsters an opportunity to learn to read and play music in a structured setting, rather than the haphazard way in which musical training was handed down until now. The fourth association concerned with entertainment is the theatrical group. Members perform plays and short skits, sometimes written by local villagers, but more often well-known religious or historical works. Theater was a particularly popular form of entertainment in times of economic hardship, for it offered a chance for all interested villagers to participate in a recreational activity at almost no expense. Moreover, all four villages generally held performances over the course of the summer which were widely attended by all residents of the Lötschental, creating a pleasant break in the routine.

Other associations are concerned primarily with masculine forms of recreation. The hunters' club is a loose-knit group of men who are avid hunters, while the

The "Alpenrose," the village band.

shooting club is a more tightly structured association, primarily because of the ties it maintains with the military. Every able-bodied man is required to fire a certain number of rounds of ammunition in target practice during the course of the year as part of his overall military obligation, and it is through the shooting club that this obligation is fulfilled. Two other male groups are the Ski Club and the *Katholische Turnverein* (Catholic gymnastic association), rival sports clubs within the village which oppose each other in all sports activities.

Additional voluntary groups are centered around the church, extending ties among various segments of the congregation. The young men are linked together in an association, as are the young girls; in each case the duties of the group are minimal, and they are usually only called together for church-related projects, such as spring cleaning in the church and cemetery. Another religious association is the *Jungmannschaftverein*, whose membership consists of young boys from primary school to marriage. The purpose of this association is to promote solidarity among the young men of the village, primarily by organizing celebrations and spare time activities to keep them busy and out of mischief. They generally meet monthly, and their schedule includes lectures and discussions as well as more active affairs. Yet another religious association is the *Altarsakramentsbruderschaft*, or the brotherhood of the sacrament of the altar. This is a ceremonial society solely for funerals, with no other church function than to accompany the corpse to the grave. The members used to wear white hooded robes, but this costume has long since been discarded, having been banned by the priest in 1912. Membership in the association is restricted to men, but any male parishioner may join with no other restrictions.

One final association deserves mention, and that is the mountain guides. The *Bergführerverein* originated some 50 years ago, and aside from bringing together men with a common interest, it has a more formal role in regulating entrance into its ranks and establishing fixed rates for the many tours in and near the Lötschental. The local chapter of this association is made up of men from all four villages, and is affiliated with other chapters in Valais and throughout Switzerland.

Young men dressed in traditional costumes at pre-Lenten festival. (Photo by Albert Nyfeler, courtesy of Professor Arnold Niederer)

Tschäggättä, *the traditional mask worn during pre-Lenten festivities.*

All along we have stressed the relative economic equality of Kippel residents, particularly in the prewar agro-pastoral era. But does this imply a social equality as well? To a certain extent this is the case, although I shall point out some minor differences within the village, and more major social distances beyond the village boundaries.

Prior to the war, almost every employed male in the village worked in agriculture. The Swiss National Census gives the following figures:

In 1910—128 of 154 total employed, or 83.1%
In 1920—150 of 177 total employed, or 84.7%
In 1930—128 of 156 total employed, or 82.1%

Unfortunately the census figures are unclear, for they do not describe exactly what various occupational categories include. The figures for agriculturalists should probably be considered on the low side, however, for a man too poor to live entirely from his own landholding and who therefore worked part time as a day laborer or seasonal worker outside the valley was classified as industrial, or other nonagricultural. Yet several men who did this retained their meager holding within the valley, and generally their wives and families carried out the agricultural tasks while they were away—without agriculture they could not have survived. Since most families relied upon agriculture, they were therefore strictly tied in with the reigning subsistence economy of the Lötschental at that time. Most men who worked outside the valley and brought in some cash were otherwise so poor that their cash did not give them an economic advantage, but rather barely brought them up to the subsistence level. It is clear that for most families status was based upon agricultural wealth; that is the amount of various kinds of land, number of buildings, cattle and other animals, implements, etc. But since the Lötschental was economically not well off until some time after the war, social stratification was often based upon very subtle differences as to the relative state of poverty of a family.

There are, however, a few exceptions to the rule of status based on agricultural success. Certain individuals who held special positions within the village, and who received a cash income for their services, ranked as the village elite. The priest, the postman, and the teacher were the main figures of this type in the prewar days, the postman receiving his salary from the federal government, the other two from the villagers themselves. Although cash incomes were never very high, the supplemental cash did not restrict these individuals from pursuing full-scale agricultural activities as well, particularly since they had the means available to them. The priest was able to obtain the yield from church-owned lands, while the postman and teacher, both natives of the valley, had their inheritance and their wife's to support them. Their cash went a long way during these hard times, and it served to raise them in the system of stratification within the village.

The priest hardly figures in an overall ranking system, however, for he had no private property and therefore he stood out as an individual, separate from the rest of the villagers. The other two, along with a couple of men who worked full time outside the valley, commuting perhaps weekly or even monthly, were at the top of the social ladder. The rest were ranked according to agricultural wealth. Village officials obtained increased prestige and higher status for their tenure of office, but since most positions rotated on a regular basis, this was only a temporary elevation.

The rankings in such a system of social stratification, based upon achieved rather than ascribed status, upon primarily economic rather than social criteria, were not transferred from generation to generation. The position of teacher was not hereditary, nor was that of postman necessarily so, although in this case it happened that the son of the first postman took over his father's position. Agricultural wealth could disappear within a generation through the system of partible inheritance, just as a propitious marriage could raise the status of an entire family overnight. Opportunity for limited social mobility within the confines of Kippel was certainly not lacking, although upper limits were low in comparison with the world outside. Marriage was perhaps the most common means of increasing status, but it was not always easy to marry into a wealthy family. If a prosperous villager had many children he would have to limit the number of those who married in order to maintain his wealth, thereby limiting the number of opportunities for others to share in his prosperity. If, on the other hand, he had but one or two children, he could be quite selective as to whom they married, or rather they could be selective themselves, for they would certainly be sought after.

Another avenue of mobility within the system of social ranking of Kippel was education, primarily as a prerequisite to a career as a teacher if one wished to remain in Kippel, or else to qualify one for high paying, high prestige employment outside the valley. Education, however, was limited in that it required that a family be able to sacrifice a member of its labor force. The economic situation being what it was before the war, this was highly unlikely. Moreover, education beyond the primary school level required that the student leave the valley, and rarely could a Lötschental family support one of its members outside the household.

Emigration offered another opportunity for mobility either outside the valley, in which case the emigrant's family reflected a portion of the prestige accrued by the emigrant in his new location, or even possibly within the valley in the infrequent case of an emigrant returning to the Lötschental after a profitable absence. The most popular reason for emigrating was to join the Swiss Papal Guard in the Vatican. Here a man needed only to serve for fifteen years, after which he was retired with a pension. Many men from the Lötschental followed this course, and returned to marry a local girl (service in the Guard is only open to unmarried men). They could then live out the rest of their lives in relative comfort, with an average agricultural holding and a sizable cash income on top of it.

Ties between emigrants and their relatives in the valley were frequently strong, but were socially rather than economically oriented. If the emigrant remained in Switzerland, particularly in Valais, he could return often to the Lötschental for a vacation, thus renewing his contact and reinforcing the kinship bonds he had in his home village. Rarely, however, did a Lötschentaler reciprocate by visiting a relative in the city. So the relationship was one of the emigrant to his home village more than one of mutual ties among kin or friends. The prestige of a city relative only applied within the Lötschental when the individual was known there, that is, when he returned frequently.

Group status relative to the outside world was both a social and an economic phenomenon. Within the Lötschental Kippel considered itself to be at the top of the social ladder, not so much for economic reasons, but more out of regard for its being the religious center of the valley. Of course the other villages had similar ideas about their own superiority, and intervillage rivalry was always keen.

Kippel vis-à-vis the outside world was another story. The Swiss form of government, which grants a certain autonomy to every commune regardless of size or importance, imbues every citizen with a feeling of equality. Social stratification of large groups must then take another basis, rather than an inherent social or legal difference among citizens. In most cases the criterion chosen is wealth, although education and cosmopolitan sophistication are also important, perhaps not independent of wealth. In Switzerland the overall tendency is to look down upon the residents of the mountain cantons as poor mountain peasants, the "country bumpkins" of Switzerland. In Valais, one of the poorest mountain cantons, people tend to look down upon the Lötschental as one of the poorest, least sophisticated regions of the canton. The people of the Lötschental recognize this, and react in two ways. They have developed a value system accenting their strong points, which they apply to themselves and others at the same time, and subsequently use to rank themselves high on the social ladder, based upon their own criteria. Hard work, honesty, communal spirit, strong religious conviction— with these standards they consider themselves superior to the city dweller, despite their poverty and simple life. These values are reinforced by the local church, which instills a pride in their way of life, in an effort to maintain it rather than drive people to the cities and perhaps out of the arms of the church.

The second way in which they combat their negative image in the rest of the canton is by emphasizing the negative aspects of other groups which could conceivably be considered even lower in the system of stratification, primarily the Italians, but also other ethnic and religious groups depending upon the context. If the consideration is merely within the German region of Valais, then the French-speaking people of Lower Valais provide an ideal scapegoat for all the economic ills of the canton, for indeed the French outnumber the Germans in Valais, and their stereotyped laziness and lack of industry are used to indicate their responsibility for this situation. If instead the discussion is within a religious context, then it is a question of the Jews, or sometimes even the Protestants, or all non-Roman Catholics, who are to be considered socially inferior. At times this quest for social status approaches a point of almost blind bigotry as a means of reinforcing the tenuous positive self-image. Yet considering the types of contact an inhabitant of the Lötschental has with outsiders, this attitude is not altogether unaccountable. When he deals with them outside his home area he is often confused and taken advantage of. When, on the other hand, they come to the Lötschental as visitors, he is shocked by their ignorance and insensitivity to his way of life. He develops a negative image of all foreigners, and transfers his frustration and anxiety to those most vulnerable because of their economic situation or their religion, such as the Italians or the non-Catholics.

5 / Industrialization after World War II

The period following World War II saw a broad economic transformation throughout the canton of Valais. A new emphasis was placed upon industrialization in the rural mountain cantons, and the "politics of industry" fostered rapid development in the areas of transportation, water power and other forms of energy, and metals and chemicals. Between 1950 and 1964 the number of factories in Valais increased from 115 to 252, while the total employed in them rose from 6294 to 13,078 (Kaufmann 1965:106).

At the same time, whereas Valaisan agriculture had thrived during the war because of the closed borders preventing importation of inexpensive fruits and vegetables from neighboring Italian markets, after the war this was no longer the case. With the lifting of trade restrictions, Valais farmers could no longer compete with the cheaper labor and reduced prices of imported goods, and an agricultural crisis ensued. The commercial farmers in the Rhone Valley were forced to become more specialized and highly competitive, driving the small producer into the factory for his livelihood. Peasant agriculture for subsistence could only be retained where the land had little value and production was still mainly for consumption. Even then, as the rural areas became drawn into the cash economy the peasant found he had to rely more and more on money which grew increasingly difficult to obtain through agriculture.

Thus the broad economic change in Valais filtered out into the subsidiary valleys indirectly, in that reliance upon the cash economy spread at the same time that agriculture ceased to provide a source of income. Prior to World War II money had been relatively unimportant in the subsistence economy of the Lötschental; it was used occasionally outside the valley, but transactions in the daily lives of the villagers were based almost exclusively upon reciprocation and barter. The economics of self-sufficiency as it was practiced in the Lötschental did not require a steady source of cash incomes—what little the people needed they could raise by selling an animal or some dairy products, or perhaps the product of a home industry.

Of course, the residents of Kippel and the other villages in the Lötschental were not totally ignorant of the pleasures of money. The railroad line had broken down communication barriers and introduced the villagers to consumer goods available from outside the valley. Moreover, both world wars provided many local residents with steady, if meager, incomes. The fuel shortage created by restrictions on trade led to the opening of an anthracite coal mine near Ferden. Normally unable to yield a profit, the mine became necessary during the war years of 1914–18 and 1939–45, and a number of valley residents, mostly women and children, were employed there while the men were off with the army securing the borders and maintaining a ready reserve force on alert.

It was the general industrialization of the canton, however, that was important for the postwar economy of the Lötschental. Certainly the changeover from a barter to a money economy was a gradual process, just as it was a sporadic one. The use of money can be traced back many centuries, yet it did not begin to dominate the valley economy until very recently—the second world war is chosen as the turning point not because of anything that occurred inside the valley as a direct result of the war, but because of what happened in the entire canton of Valais, and particularly in the Rhone Valley beginning after 1945. The changing

Cultivation with traditional implements, such as the broad hoe, continues today.

The scythe is still used to cut hay.

emphasis upon cash, and more important the creation of a perceived need for it, would not have had the effect it had without a source of employment. The industrialization of Valais created that employment potential, and the residents of the lateral subsidiary valleys, the former rural mountain peasants, left their farms and went to work in the factories.

Sharpening a scythe with a whetstone.

OCCUPATIONAL CHANGE, 1945–1960

The population of the Lötschental had grown steadily throughout the first four decades of the century. Kippel alone had gone from 248 in 1900 to 340 in 1941, an increase of 37.1 percent. Agriculture expanded to the point where every available square foot of land was utilized, but the land was poor and the per capita production declined. A few people were able to emigrate, but the Depression hit the cities harder than the rural areas, and jobs were few and far between; at least one had a little land and hopefully enough to eat if one stayed home and worked in agriculture.

This was the situation when the postwar industrial boom opened up new opportunities for the rural Valaisan peasantry. Many young people were forced to find work, either because of the overcrowding of their village and their farm-

One of the few remaining farmers in the village.

land, or else to help support their families. The typical family in the Lötschental was quite large, and parents were frequently driven into debt in order to support their children, particularly in the lean years just prior to the war. Thus when the children reached the age where they could go out and earn a cash income, and more important when there were cash incomes to be earned, they became more valuable to the family outside the valley than at home, where they would just be another mouth to feed. Extra agricultural labor was not necessary, and cash debts had to be paid in hard currency.

In the early stages of industrialization the majority of the positions open to unskilled, untrained rural workers were as manual laborers. This of course meant that the mobility of the work force was strictly limited, for the families could not afford to provide their children with an education, and specialized apprentice-ships and training programs had not yet been developed in an area where industry was so new. Most of the men took jobs in construction projects, either on water power projects or factories; many men from Kippel worked at the construction of the dam for the Grand Dixence project, which employed over 1500 workers at its peak (Kaufmann 1965:137).

Of 120 men from the Lötschental born between 1920–1929, which would place them directly in the postwar work force, 25 percent learned some sort of skilled labor; 19.2 percent were trained to be semiskilled workers, some of them forced to accept a more immediate source of income even though they had sought a position as an apprentice to a skilled craftsman; and 55.8 percent were un-skilled workers, many of whom had also expressed a desire to learn a trade but were unable to do so because of the financial demands upon them and their families. Of 117 girls in the same age bracket, only 8.5 percent were skilled, 56.4 percent semiskilled (including hotel work), and the remaining 35.1 percent unskilled (Hallenbarter 1946:14–18).

The census for the years 1941–1960 indicates the change in the occupational structure of the village, as agriculture gave way to industry as the main source of support.

	1941	1950	1960
Total Employed	160	144	151
Agriculture	122	102	55
%	76.3	70.8	36.4
Industry	7	14	63
%	4.4	9.7	41.7
Commerce, Hotels, etc.	31	28	33
%	19.3	19.5	21.9

At the outset of the war, agriculture clearly dominated the village economy, with more than three-fourths of the work force engaged in some form of agro-pastoralism. In 1950 the movement away from agriculture to industry had not yet begun, and the occupational distribution was much the same as it had been prior to the war. It was not until after 1950 that the men from Kippel began to flock to the Rhone Valley seeking work first in construction, then in the factories, water power plants, and the transportation network they had helped to build. A wide variety of men made up the Kippel contingent of the rural labor force—married sons who were still awaiting their inheritance and thus were not tied down to agriculture, frustrated farmers who either could not make a living from their land or who still harbored bitter memories of the poverty of the 1930s, younger sons who were squeezed out by the population explosion or whose inheritance was not enough to support an agricultural operation, and young men simply seeking adventure outside the valley. Some of these men commuted home regularly to see their families, while others went back less frequently. Still others never did return, the lure of the outside world being too great. More important, all of them had made the initial break with agriculture, and this was to have its effect upon the economy of the valley.

EMERGENCE OF THE WORKER–PEASANT

Clearly with the bulk of the labor force leaving the village and agriculture for industrial jobs in the Rhone Valley, commuting back and forth whenever possible, the agricultural output of the village declined in the period following World War II. Between 1939 and 1955, according to the agricultural census, the number of cattle pastured on the alps in Kippel declined from 183 to 115, a drop of 37.2 percent. This is a particularly significant figure, since cattle are the center of the mixed agro-pastoral alpine economy, providing an index not only of the dairy production but of the agricultural labor involved in planting and harvesting supplementary fodder crops and hay.

Yet agriculture did not disappear entirely. The men who gave up farming and went to work in the factories still retained a small agricultural operation for their household use—they were willing to give up agriculture as a source of livelihood, but not as a way of life. The result was a growing class of what have been called worker–peasants (*Arbeiterbauer*), industrial laborers who manage a small-scale farm for their private use in their spare time. Even in the prewar days, the concept of the worker-peasant was known in the Lötschental, although it was applied somewhat differently. Whereas in the postwar era the men worked in factories, using the advantage of a swing shift schedule (mornings one week, evenings the next, nights the next, etc.) to work their land, earlier there were no factory jobs. The worker–peasant in the prewar era was a man who found supplementary irregular work as a manual laborer during the slack periods in his agricultural cycle, in order to add to his income. The main difference is that the more recent worker–peasant lives primarily from his factory wages and treats his agriculture as a secondary occupation, while the prewar man lived from agriculture and his outside earnings were merely brought in to enable him to support his family on an otherwise insufficient amount of land. In fact, if a man were well off, that is if he owned enough land and animals to get by on, he probably would not seek wage labor outside the valley at all.

The farming operation of the postwar worker–peasant was obviously not as intensive as it had been when all the labor of the entire household could be concentrated upon it. Working an eight hour day left a man little time to attend to the daily chores, let alone the major demands of planting and harvest. One result was the decline in productivity, with fewer cattle to support and more cash

Gathering the hay harvest.

Carrying hay from the fields to the barn.

available for consumer items and food. Home industry was rapidly replaced by manufactured goods imported from outside the valley. A second result was a greater reliance upon the women in the household to perform the necessary labor to keep the farm going. The women had always participated to some extent, caring for the cattle and helping out at planting and harvest, or working at other odd jobs such as threshing. But with the absence of the man for the greater part of the work day the wife and children, and even the parents if they lived with the family, were called upon to make up for the loss in labor. Of course there was less total labor involved, but proportionately more for the rest of the family, especially the wife. The men usually were able to perform the heaviest work, however, either by scheduling their vacations to coincide with the harvest season, or else simply by staying home from work or putting in an extra long day when necessary. High rates of absenteeism and industrial accidents in the factories coincide with the busiest agricultural seasons, indicating the effect that the agricultural cycle has upon the worker.

A number of other changes in the traditional balance of the agricultural operation also reflect the impact of factory work. The pattern of livestock raising shifted away from cattle, which required a great input of labor both directly in their daily care, and indirectly in the provision of hay and other food for them for the long winter in the stall; instead sheep became more popular, since they require relatively little care and they eat less. They can be left alone during the summer, which frees the women from staying on the alp to milk the cows and make butter and cheese, and during the winter they need be fed only once daily, whereas cattle are fed twice. Moreover, their wool can be sold annually, and they provide a good source of meat, either for consumption or sale. For these reasons, the worker–peasant has shifted from cattle to sheep, for he has less time to devote to livestock than formerly. A comparison of the animal counts for Kippel in 1946 and a decade later in 1956 bears out this change: the number of cattle in the village increased from 136 to 138 over that period. However, the number of people who owned cattle dropped from 45 to 33, indicating the decline in their popularity among worker–peasants; at the same time, the sheep population rose from 75 to 123.

As agriculture declined, land use patterns changed. No longer was every available piece of land needed to feed the overpopulated village—with the new source of nonagricultural income overpopulation ceased to be a problem and the amount of land cultivated or harvested declined to the point where worker-peasants who had little time to spare could be more selective about which parcels they used. Rental became more common, as the demand for land decreased. With a reevaluation of time the location and access of a field grew more important than its yield. Along with the change in land use, agricultural buildings tended to lose or change their function. One of the first things to be given up was growing enough grain for bread, for the process was simply too time-consuming and commercial flour was relatively inexpensive to buy. Most people gave up baking bread altogether, but at least they stopped cultivating rye and wheat. This of course meant that the granary fell into disuse, both as a storage area and a threshing floor. Agricultural buildings in the fields also went unused, for they were bound up with an intensive type of agriculture that ceased to be practiced by the worker–peasant. Less hay was needed to feed the declining animal population, so the barns and stalls in the fields were frequently no longer necessary. The *Zugscheune*, the barn used to store the hay until winter when it could be brought into the village on sleds, was no longer important, since the storage area in the village was now sufficient to hold the hay that was needed. Furthermore, only the most accessible fields were harvested, making the transportation of the hay into the village that much easier. And finally, since land use grew less intensive, it was no longer necessary to collect manure high up on the slopes— what was gathered in the village over the winter sufficed to fertilize the nearby fields.

With all the changes in land use patterns, it is not surprising that the annual cycle bears little resemblance to what it used to be before the war. The elimination of the practice of moving the cattle from stall to stall during the winter to avoid transporting the hay and manure is perhaps the best example. Likewise, bringing the hay down to the village has become an autumn task with a tractor and trailer, rather than a winter task with a sled. New patterns of labor and a new division of labor by age and sex also reflect the changes in land use and annual cycle. The introduction of a limited amount of agricultural machinery has also affected the work patterns in Kippel. The most common machine is a small tractor, to which a low flatbed trailer is frequently attached for hauling hay or manure. Mowing machines are useful for cutting hay on flat ground, but are relatively ineffective on steep slopes.

Rounding out the change in the agricultural sphere is the decline in communal labor, due to the increasing absence of the work force from the village. Community projects originated out of necessity, when all men were farmers and had to rely upon each other for support in order to overcome the environmental barriers and to make a living from the land. With a growing proportion of the men now engaged in nonagricultural pursuits, interest in agricultural problems is dying out. The spontaneity surrounding many projects no longer is possible, with so few men working in the fields, and planned programs must take into consideration the fact that a sizable number of men will be at work almost any time of the day or night. Some communal projects have disappeared altogether, while others have had to adapt to the new practices of the industrial economy. Land owned by the community or the church used to be worked by the men of the village together; now it is rented out to the highest bidder, who uses it for his own household. Tractors and trailers have replaced the *Mannstand* in carrying wood up to the alp to build a hut, and in bringing hay down to the village from the high fields. Moving the cattle from stall to stall in the winter has been discarded completely. A few communal projects still remain, duties which have not yet been abandoned, interests which are still maintained. One such task is the continuing construction and maintenance of avalanche protection, the erection of walls and barriers above the village. Another form of communal labor not yet completely gone is the work on the alps performed by the members of the various alp associations. Even though it involves only members of the corporate group who have a clearly defined interest in the alp (since only those who use it are required to work), this form of cooperative labor is also in a state of decline. In a sense, a vicious circle is created, for as the number of men using the alp declines, the amount of work carried out also decreases, thus the usable area of the pasturage shrinks and the quality deteriorates.

AUTARKY COMPLEX

Despite the rapid industrialization of the canton of Valais and the commercialization and modernization of agriculture in the Rhone Valley, the mixed agriculture found in the Lötschental and most other lateral valleys has remained much as it was before the war, that is, it has become technologically antiquated. The failure to mechanize is in part due to the terrain and the quality of the soil, which would hardly justify a major input of capital. However, in large part the refusal to modernize agriculture in the Lötschental is due to culture lag—industry is new and modern, and agriculture is old-fashioned; the two are not to be mixed. This maintenance of a traditional system amid the adoption of new techniques in industry and new patterns of production and consumption in other areas of village life can be called an "autarky complex," or a self-sufficiency complex. It refers not only to the retention of the material culture bound up in traditional agricultural practices, but to a mentality as well. A village has lived almost wholly self-sufficient for centuries, and attempts to hang on to its self-sufficiency even after it is no longer necessary, or even advisable.

The worker–peasant still tends to think of himself primarily as a peasant rather than a worker. He schedules his vacation to coincide with harvest time, he stays away from work to watch over the birth of a calf, he loses sleep to work in the fields, and he still refers to himself unashamedly as a mountain peasant, a *Bergbauer*. He retains his system of partible inheritance, to assure his children a viable agricultural holding to support their households, as if they were going to return to the land. And the agricultural work that he performs is still oriented toward consumption by his own household, rather than specialization for the market. He defends this by asking "What should we eat in the winter if we plant our potato and grain fields with strawberries in the summer?" (Niederer 1969:292)

Thus the autarky complex inhibits innovation within the village, particularly when it is concerned with agricultural activity. A clear example of this aspect of culture lag is seen in the crops planted by worker–peasant families and the allocations of necessary labor. Potatoes and vegetables are the most common crops, not because they are economically the soundest investment of time and money that the family can make, but because people have been doing it for so long (particularly potatoes) and because these products serve as staples in the diet. They do not think in terms of buying them, even though it might be cheaper in the long run—it would probably be an embarrassment to a family that considered itself a farming unit. Similarly at harvest time there are several families in the village who have given up all their animals yet go out and harvest their fields. Since they sell the hay to other villagers with animals, and since the price of hay is extremely low, it cannot possibly be assumed that this is a rational economic activity—certainly anyone with enough time and energy to harvest hay fields should be able to find a better way of earning more money. But it is not a question of money, so much as basic mental outlook. The fields are property owned by the family, property that has been used for centuries, and from which an income has been derived. To let that property lay fallow is wasteful, more wasteful even than taking time off from work to harvest it and sell the yield for a pittance. In one case a man rented a piece of land to another villager, and when the latter found he was not able to harvest the hay on time, the owner sent his son out to cut the hay. This attitude toward the land and the traditional agricultural practices associated with it is the kernel of the autarky complex.

SUMMARY: SOCIAL CHANGE, 1945–1960

The prime recipient of the newfound wealth of Valais was the Rhone Valley itself, and although a few projects did manage to trickle into the subsidiary valleys, notably water power developments, for the most part the more isolated villages and valleys fell even farther behind. The most important factor in this respect was the location of the factories. Although isolated villages might have been able to offer better deals in terms of taxes and land costs, they could not compete with the main valley where it really counted, in transportation and central location for the labor force. Thus there were two opposite trends acting on the subsidiary valleys at the same time. On the one hand there was the incredibly rapid, snowballing change brought about by the industrialization of the main valley. On the other hand, the gap was widened between the conservative, isolated peasant villages and the industrial towns. Despite the modernization in the industrial sector, the peasant retained his traditional agriculture and it continued to influence his village life.

Peasant villages changed much less rapidly than industrial towns, yet it was inevitable that industry would eventually draw the rural labor force into the factories, for agriculture grew less feasible as the reliance upon cash and integration into the money economy increased. Frequently occupational change led to emigration from the subsidiary valleys into the Rhone Valley, but in many more cases workers were able to commute weekly or even daily. Strong ties to the land, reinforced by the system of partible inheritance, made this a common occurrence in rural Valais, and the Lötschental was no exception.

The figures below show emigration out of the valley from Kippel, according to ten-year intervals:

1900–1909	9
1910–1919	8
1920–1929	9
1930–1939	14
1940–1949	14
1950–1959	36
1960–1969	36

Although we might expect a slightly higher rate in the 1930s and 1940s because of the effects of overpopulation coupled with a limited agricultural output, the rapid rise in emigration in the 1950s indicates a different factor, namely the availability of employment and the mobility of the new industrial economy. Nevertheless a number of men who did change over from agriculture to industry were able to remain in the village and commute to work, and they had a profound effect upon the social and economic life of their fellow villagers.

One of the most direct effects that industrialization has had upon Kippel is in the rising standard of living. In the area of housing, for example, newer, more modern and better equipped houses have been built since the war, financed at first by the increase in income through industrial labor. The importation of fruits and vegetables during the winter and cheese all year round has made the traditional diet more healthy. Medical services have become more readily available, and one of the primary indicators of the overall standard of living, the infant mortality rate, has dropped considerably since the prewar era, as the following figures show:

	Births	Infant Deaths	Rate per 1000 Births
1900–1909	93	23	247
1910–1919	80	18	225
1920–1929	74	9	122
1930–1939	67	6	90
1940–1949	110	7	64
1950–1959	96	5	52
1960–1969	97	4	41

The steady drop in the infant mortality rate, by a factor of six in this century alone, has undoubtedly had an effect upon the rate of growth of the population of Kippel and the Lötschental.

It is not surprising that with the rapid change in the occupational structure of the village, the system of social stratification within the village changed somewhat in the period following World War II. In the prewar era the village elite consisted of a trio of salaried officials—the priest, the schoolteacher, and the postman. In the 1950s most families had at least one male earning a cash income, and the basis for ranking no longer held true. Young men were able to earn money and gain their independence without necessarily waiting until they had come into their inheritance. This gave them a freedom which their parents had not had, and put them in a stronger position with regard to village affairs: they could participate as equals perhaps a decade younger than their fathers.

A host of other changes began to occur with the decline of agriculture and the substitution of industry as the basis of the village economy following the war, but many of them did not really come into prominence until much later. The 1960s saw a number of results of changes that had begun in the previous decade, just as the 1970s promise to carry on the trends of the 1960s. It took about a decade for the results of the shift of the village labor force to the more mobile industrial sector to become evident—children were freed from the drudgery and time-consuming nature of agricultural labor and an industrial world view began to take shape to match the occupational structure. These and other postwar changes in the social and economic life of Kippel will be discussed in detail in the next chapter.

6 / Modernization since 1960

In most discussions of social change a number of processes are generally assumed to be related, so that we tend to view modernization as encompassing industrialization, urbanization, and westernization, whatever that is taken to mean. We look back to the history of the Industrial Revolution in England and the United States and see it occurring in the context of cities, and we watch it as it transforms the nature of the average citizen to conform to the model of industrial man. The mistake we make is that we view this process as one in time and space, although in reality it occurred in stages over a long period of time and is still continuing in ways we do not always comprehend. This mistake is carried over to our study of industrialization in other countries since the initial revolution more than two centuries ago.

This short study of a village and the transformations it has undergone in less than a quarter of a century offers a clear and concise contradiction to some of the common assumptions we make about modernization and industrialization. First of all, industrialization need not coincide with urbanization, for as we have seen, the economy of the village and the life style of the villagers became industrialized without transforming Kippel into a large metropolis or a seat of rural industry. The men and women commute to work, and even the towns where they work are small and in many ways rustic. Secondly, we find that industrialization and modernization are not the same thing, and they do not necessarily occur together—one might question whether in fact they ever really occur together. Industrialization in Kippel is a process that began shortly after World War II, the initial stages of which lasted between 10 and 15 years. Modernization, or, as I see it, the adaptation of basic social institutions to an economy based upon the secondary and tertiary sectors (industry and services) rather than agriculture, is a process which in Kippel has only really begun on any meaningful scale in the last decade, well after industrial employment had firmly established itself with the villagers. But the economy has not stood still while Kippel caught up with it. The economic base of the village has already begun to change again from industry to tourism, and the worker–peasant has had to yield to the specialist, the trained and educated man of tomorrow. This chapter will deal with two separate aspects of life in Kippel: the modernization that had its beginnings perhaps 25 years ago but which shifted into high gear less than ten years ago, and the second stage in the transformation of the economy. The two aspects cannot easily be separated, which as we shall see sometimes leads to a most interesting situation: the man of today trying to adjust to yesterday and tomorrow at the same time.

OCCUPATIONAL CHANGE, 1960–1970

In the 1950s the trend in occupational change was out of agriculture into industry. According to the census figures in 1960 the flow out of agriculture in Kippel was just over 30 percent, from 70.8 percent in 1950 to 36.4 percent in 1960, which matched the rise in industrial labor, from 9.7 percent in 1950 to 41.7 percent in 1960. After the major construction projects were completed, most of the men continued to work in industry, in unskilled or semiskilled factory jobs, in the construction industry elsewhere, or perhaps for the railroad. About this time a major aluminum factory was built in the village of Steg, located at the mouth of the Lötschental in the Rhone Valley. In 1961 the factory was completed and several men took jobs there; by 1970 the work force from Kippel had grown to twenty. These men represent the last of the worker–peasantry in Kippel, for the aluminum factory was the last major source of unskilled industrial labor to tap the manpower of the Lötschental. The men were able to settle in their home villages and commute daily to work, which enabled them to take up agriculture once again as a sideline occupation, making use of the land they inherited.

Despite the effects of the aluminum factory, the shift in the occupational structure of the village in the 1960s did not parallel that of the previous decade. Agriculture continued to decline, but the flow was not into industry, but rather into commerce, transportation, and other service-oriented jobs, as the following figures indicate:

	1950	1960	1970
Total Employed	144	151	190
Agriculture	102	55	27
%	70.8	36.4	14.2
Industry	14	63	60
%	9.7	41.7	31.6
Commerce, Hotels, etc.	28	33	103
%	19.5	21.9	54.2

The continued drop in agricultural employment was not unexpected, but it was combined with a decline in industrial jobs, in favor of service positions. With the rise in the average income in the industrial labor of the 1950s and the consequent deemphasis on agricultural labor, young boys were released from the responsibilities of farm work. Furthermore, they were not saddled with the debts of their families as soon as they finished the required schooling, which meant they were free to seek additional training, rather than going directly into agriculture or having to provide for their family.

Thus within one generation a second wave of occupational change occurred. The first wave followed the second world war, when industrial jobs were created and many men from Kippel left agriculture to fill them. Their sons were thereby freed from their financial responsibilities, and beginning about 1960 they made use of this freedom by seeking more training to prepare themselves for skilled positions as mechanics, electricians, and the like, or in nonindustrial jobs as white collar workers such as draftsmen, salesmen, or bank tellers. This "occupational generation gap," as I call it, is represented in the figures below, which give the occupation of Kippel residents by age in 1970:

Age Group	Total	Agriculture		Industry		Skilled Tradesman, Commerce, Professional	
		number	percent	number	percent	number	percent
15–34	61	2	3.3	7	11.5	52	85.2
35–54	35	0	–	23	65.7	12	34.3
55 up	27	12	44.4	7	25.9	8	29.7

Today in Kippel there are only two young men engaged in agriculture. One is a full time farmer, the son of the largest landowner, who plans to make a living from farming, while the other is a dropout from a trade school who returned to the village to help his father on the family holding. If he should go into agriculture once he takes over the family farm, it would be the result not so much of a conscious choice as of the elimination of other possibilities.

One gets a better picture of the nature of the division by age of the occupational structure of the village in the diagram on page 93, which shows male occupations in Kippel by age in 1970. In effect, this diagram is a concise history of the village—the old men are farmers, the middle-aged men are unskilled worker–peasants, and the youngsters are skilled tradesmen, white collar workers, and commercial rather than industrial workers. These three categories reflect the three economic stages of the village and the valley in the last thirty years.

A slightly larger percentage of young women are engaged in agriculture, 11 of them under thirty-five years of age. Mostly the daughters of either the older full-time farmers or the middle-aged worker–peasants, they serve as helpers in the agricultural operation, as the majority of the work continues to fall upon the shoulders of the women in the household. They will undoubtedly give up their status as farm girls when they marry, or else when they find they are unable to run the family operation alone after their fathers have grown too old to work. A large number of young girls work in factories at unskilled jobs, or in hotels or other service-oriented positions, indicating the heavy emphasis in upbringing

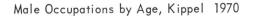

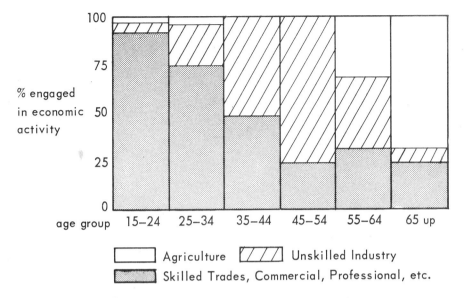

Male Occupations by Age, Kippel 1970

% engaged in economic activity

age group

Agriculture   Unskilled Industry
Skilled Trades, Commercial, Professional, etc.

upon the role of a woman as a housekeeper, wife, and mother. There is little occupational mobility through continued education or specialized training: factory work is acceptable and even desirable for a girl to earn money before she is married, but in most cases higher education is considered a waste of time.

The number of jobs in Kippel and in the Lötschental for Kippel residents has increased, offering many men and women an opportunity to earn their living in their home village. Four men from Kippel are chauffeurs for the postal bus service which carries mail and passengers within the Lötschental; two men run a knitting factory in Kippel (there are five such factories in the neighboring village of Wiler), which also employs several women full time and offers piecework to many more women in their homes in order to bring in extra income. A number of stores and restaurant/bars offer employment to local residents. Seasonal income is available for mountain guides and ski instructors, as well as the two men required to operate the chair lift from Kippel to Hockenalp. Finally, there is the tradition of mask carving which has recently become popular as an additional source of income. Miniature replicas of wooden masks used in traditional festivals are sold to tourists throughout the valley and are even distributed to outlets in nearby towns in the Rhone Valley. These sources of income are all in addition to those which existed prior to 1960, including a plumber, carpenter, baker, teacher, shoemaker, tailor, and, of course, the clergymen.

Home industry in Kippel has declined, unable to compete with the piecework offered by the local knitting factories. Home manufacturing simply is not adapted to a cash income and the specialization it implies. Almost every household in Kippel today has at least one woman doing part-time work for a knitting factory to bring in extra cash; in many cases the factory owner even delivers a machine to the woman's house so that she may work at home without severely disrupting her routine. Most women do finishing work on factory-knitted articles, adding buttons, binding seams, or contributing decorative touches.

DECLINE OF THE WORKER–PEASANT

Agriculture as a sole source of support for a family in Kippel is a thing of the past—today there is not one household that lives entirely off its agricultural holding without an outside source of income, be it merely wages from a local knitting factory. A few families have remained primarily in agriculture, while most have gone the way of the worker–peasant. Households that have given up most of their agriculture still can claim a small income through the sale of wool, if they have sheep, or hay, if they have no animals at all.

Given the relatively rapid industrialization of Valais and its penetration into the Lötschental, it is no wonder that agriculture is declining. The mountain peasants continue to demand more from the cantonal and federal officials if they are to follow the government-supported policy of maintaining an agricultural foothold in the mountains, and while it is true that the benefits continue to go up, villagers complain that it is never enough. Whereas the factory worker receives a monthly pay check, the farmer receives no regular payment except the quarterly allowance for dependent children. His income is irregular, a problem in this age of the money economy. Despite subsidies for machinery, the mountain peasant cannot mechanize because there are too many ecological limitations. He has no regular free time—something increasingly in demand among the younger generation. If he has cattle, he must care for them every day; he has no security if he becomes ill. He has little to do in the winter, but during the summer he is forced to work long hours every day. All this adds up to a preference for regular and better paying work. The only people left in agriculture are old, and their number is dwindling rapidly. The younger family members are no longer willing to assume the tasks involved in maintaining an agricultural operation, and so the old men are selling out, giving up, and retiring. As one man said, "Agriculture today is just a hobby, something for the old men to do to pass the time."

This severe and rapid decline in agriculture has created problems for those who have remained in it, since they can no longer rely upon the communal efforts of their fellow villagers in their battle against the steep terrain and unfavorable environment. They have had to give in to the money economy even though they remain in agriculture, for wage labor has replaced the traditional cooperative projects, and the tractor and trailer must be used in place of the *Mannstand*. The largest landowner in Kippel still grows a little wheat and barley as extra feed for his cows, but he has for the most part changed over to purchasing feed supplements. He claims that even the second hay cutting is becoming a rarity in most fields, with the use of manure and even commercial fertilizer declining. Instead animal owners today frequently prefer to purchase hay from their fellow villagers when possible, or from the outside rather than harvest it themselves. As one old farmer commented while watching a truckload of hay being unloaded in the village square, "In the old days it used to be all right if a person bought food for his family, but if he had to buy food for his 'family in the stall' he wouldn't last long." Today almost everyone with cattle buys food supplements, if not hay as well, and in the long run it probably pays off with better milk and larger and healthier animals.

In this respect we see the breakdown of the autarky complex and a decline in the worker–peasantry, as men come to realize that their time and labor now has more value and they are more rational about their expenditure of both. At the same time it is becoming obvious that the more agriculture diminishes, the less possible it will be to keep it up, for it depends too much upon continual maintenance, not to mention communal effort. Self-sufficiency is being recognized as a function of the entire village economy, not just of individual household agricultural practices. The decline of the autarky complex is beginning to show up in the use of buildings. The poor physical condition of many granaries and storage sheds testifies to the fact that they are not as important as they used to be; were this not the case, people would be more likely to invest in their repair and maintenance (Bachmann 1970:337).

According to the annual counts made in the village for cattle, and to a count I made with the help of a villager for sheep and goats in 1970, the cattle and goat populations are continuing to decline while sheep number just about the same. In 1968 25 men owned 101 cattle as compared to 28 men owning 101 in 1966. The next year there were still 25 owners but only 95 cattle in the village, and in 1970 24 men owned only 87 head. As for smaller animals, the number of owners fell from 14 in 1966 to 10 in 1970, and the total herd of goats in the village dropped from 37 to 21. The decline in the number of cattle has hit the alps particularly hard. In 1965 there were 52 cows on Hockenalp owned by 19 different men. One owner dropped out in 1966, another in 1967, and by 1970 there were only 14 owners represented on the alp, with a total of 37 cows.

The typical reason given for withdrawing from participation in the alpine grazing period is the lack of personnel to tend the cattle while they are on the high pasture. In one case a man sold all but one of his cattle, keeping one cow in a stall in the village for milk. His son explained his keeping one cow as completely irrational, then added quickly, "But you know how sentimental the old farmers are." Many others have given up their livestock completely, as it has become impossible to find young girls willing to spend their summers on the alp. This trend promises to continue in the future. One woman wanted to sell her cows and give up agriculture in 1970, but could not find a buyer in time. Another man is moving out of the valley, and although he will return in the summer, he will no longer keep his cattle here. Another old man has no younger women in his family, and his wife presently goes up to the alp. None of these people can be counted on to keep up the traditional use of the high pastures in the future. Nor can the alps eventually be leased to outsiders who require extra grazing area, at least not in their present condition. Cattle raising for profit has become a highly specialized economic activity, and summer pasturage requires large, specialized buildings. None of the alps in the Lötschental are equipped to handle the needs of outsiders, for they have grown up in response to the patterns of use of local residents, based upon their proximity to the permanent settlements. Instead, the alps are taking on a new meaning tied in with tourism. Today the alp hut has taken on a new function as a vacation house for tourists who want to "rough it" in the mountains. It is an ideal starting place for long hikes high above the valley floor, and to a lesser degree it is also suitable for winter vacations for ski enthusiasts. An entirely new meaning has thereby been added to the ownership of use-rights to the alp. Previously use-rights were primarily designed to limit grazing, and a fringe benefit included the right to build a hut for use during the summer. With tourism displacing grazing as the economic basis of the alp, the right to build a hut is now the chief value of a use-right. Already in at least one case in the Lötschental an alp right has been sold to someone who has never owned animals in the valley, but who bought it simply in order to be allowed to build a hut.

TOURISM

Tourism has been the single most important factor in the economic change in Kippel in the 1960s. It is not directly related to local industrialization, although certainly it has been facilitated by the development of a modern transportation system. Tourism has long been a tradition in the Alps; although in the Middle Ages the region was commonly considered to be inhabited by devilish spirits and frightful ghosts, with the Renaissance and the writings of Rousseau the mountains gained prominence with foreign travelers. Early tourists were treated with much suspicion by the native Valaisan inhabitants, unaccustomed as they were to contact with outsiders:

> Up until the 19th century a journey through Valais was an adventure in itself, not recommended without a sturdy mount and a trustworthy guide. The roads were in wretched condition and the local inhabitants were distrustful of strangers, often hostile. Thus the first English tourists in Zermatt were taken for thieves and sheep rustlers, and had to be rescued by the priest from the aroused villagers (Beerli 1961:247).

Kaufmann (1965:27) cites a similar tale from the Lötschental, as told by a tourist recounting his trip through the Alps in 1830:

> An old grandmother crossed herself and ran by as quickly as possible. Everywhere I saw that we were deemed capable of nothing good. In Kippel, where the priest was also the innkeeper, we were let into his house only after long deliberation with the neighbors, while we sat in uncertainty for a good half hour on the wall of the churchyard.

Tourism in the Lötschental dates back to 1868, when the Hotel Nesthorn was opened in Ried. Most early visitors were mountain climbers or members of alpine clubs, drawn to the Lötschental in the summer by the imposing Bietschhorn; transportation difficulties kept the valley closed off for much of the winter. In 1908 the Hotel Lötschberg was built in Kippel, and the Hotel Fafleralp above Blatten, and shortly thereafter the Gasthaus Kippel. When the Lötschberg Tunnel was opened in 1913, extending the railway from the Bernese Highland to Brig,

The 13,000 foot Bietschhorn, the earliest tourist attraction.

the valley was opened up to tourism—no longer was it necessary to make the long trek up from Gampel and the Rhone Valley, or over the Lötschen Pass. Hotel building continued after the first world war, and again after the second, not only in the villages but on the alps as well. Siegen notes that by 1959 there were 14 different places offering tourist accommodations, with a total of around 300 beds (1959:43). Two early monographs, *Am Lötschberg: Land und Leute von Lötschen (Land and People of the Lötschental)* written by F. G. Stebler in 1907, and *Lötschen*, by Hedwig Anneler in 1917, contributed to the reputation of the Lötschental, as did the picturesque drawings by Karl Anneler in his sister's book. Perhaps even more of an impact was made by the paintings of the artist Albert Nyfeler of Kippel, who enjoyed a wide reputation and exhibited his work throughout Switzerland.

Despite the excellent rail connections to the Lötschental, however, the valley has never relied heavily upon tourism, certainly not to the extent of other well known Valais resort areas such as Zermatt, Saas-Fee, Verbier, or Montana. In general tourism in Valais has provided capital for improvements in agriculture, particularly for investment in new, more modern methods of production. It has also altered to some extent the traditional patterns of production, introducing more commercial crops in place of subsistence products. In the Lötschental this has not been the case until very recently. Several families have been able to earn a little money by selling milk to tourists, while a few men have found seasonal employment as mountain guides or more recently as ski instructors. But full time employment for large numbers of inhabitants in the tourist industry has not been possible, and the excess population has had to look elsewhere, particularly to nearby factories, for work.

Only within the last few years has tourism grown to the point where a significant number of inhabitants of the Lötschental are able to earn a living from it. The primary force in this new economic movement has come from a British development company, which has purchased almost 50 acres of land on the northern slope above Wiler, and is in the process of developing it into a tourist resort. Part of the land is being sold to individuals (British and American) for private vacation chalets, and the rest is earmarked for a miniature town, eventually providing over 4000 beds, along with the necessary shops and entertainment facilities. The annual report of this company cites figures from the Lötschental tourist office as to the rise in tourism in the valley: according to payments of a lodging tax, the number of tourists staying in the Lötschental has risen from 29,574 to 52,710 in the short space of seven years, from 1960 to 1967. Also mentioned are figures on the number of passengers carried by the postal bus service, with an astounding increase of from 20,003 in 1951 to 130,703 in 1967.

Two major economic effects of the increase in tourism are readily apparent. The rise in the last decade, along with the projected rise due to the proposed development above Wiler, has led to a change in the occupational structure of the valley and continues to push in this direction. Local residents are eager to cash in on the new trend, and sources of income are becoming available to them within their own village. Increased demand for transportation has meant that six men are now employed by the postal bus service, four of them from Kippel. Mask carving is becoming increasingly popular, not only as a spare-time activity, but in several cases as a full time occupation. Hand carved masks selling for $2 to $100 are a favorite souvenir. More stores and taverns are able to prosper by selling supplies to tourists, and the hotel industry is increasingly successful, enabling it to employ more local residents. Plans for new development will add occupational opportunities as well. New ski lifts and chair lifts will

The parade of the Grenadiers, a traditional celebration which has become such a popular tourist attraction that it is described in the Michelin Guide.

create winter jobs to accommodate skiers. (The chair lift from Kippel to Haispiel, converted from a ski lift in 1966, carried 17,350 passengers in its first full year of operation. By 1969 the figure jumped to 28,499, and it is rapidly becoming inadequate to handle the traffic.) Other aspects of the transportation network must also be improved and increased, yielding jobs for road work and maintenance.

According to the development company representative, the resort above Wiler will be ready for use in about five years, although plans do not call for completion before ten years from now. Certainly there will be job openings in the new resort, although it is difficult to say what kind of work will be available, other than menial tasks such as tending ski lifts. Judging from the high concentra-

A new building financed by land sales to the British development company. Many of the apartments are rented to tourists.

tion of English-speaking tourists for whom this development is primarily intended, and from the attitudes of the developers concerning the inadequacy of the local population, it is fair to assume that relatively few Lötschental residents will be given high-ranking employment in the enterprise. This is not to say that the entire work force will be recruited from outside, however, for already at least two young men from Wiler have been sent by the development company to England to learn English, and plans apparently provide for the continuation of this practice.*

The second major economic effect of tourism, besides the creation of new jobs within the valley, is that in purchasing land, the investment company has poured a tremendous amount of money into the Lötschental economy. Over a dozen Kipplers have sold land to the British development company, in some cases for staggering amounts of money. The declining interest in agriculture and the financial difficulties of many families set up an ideal situation for someone with the right contacts and enough cash. Much of the "windfall" income from tourism in Kippel has gone into the construction of new houses. In one case a man built a block of eight flats at a cost of well over $100,000, with the down payment coming from land sales in Wiler. Various sources of outside aid have also played an important role in the building boom, providing inexpensive loans as part of the government policy to keep the mountain valleys populated. Rail-

---

* Since this was written I have learned that both these men have severed their ties with the development corporation, and have been replaced by English-speaking British employees.

road and postal workers are eligible for low interest building loans from the federal government, and mountain agriculturalists can qualify for cantonal funds. Most new houses were built with a speculative eye toward the tourist traffic, with the result that two- and three-family houses are occupied permanently by only one family, the other flats being rented out whenever possible. A fully furnished flat with six beds could conceivably bring in up to $90 per week during the peak tourist season, more than matching the wages of a factory worker for that same period. Since several houses have at least two extra flats (the owner's family might even move into the basement if he could rent his own flat to tourists), it is possible for a family to make in excess of $150 a week for at least ten weeks during the peak season, possibly twenty including the winter vacation period, yielding an income of $3000 from the house alone. In contrast, a laborer working for the railroad or in a factory could expect to earn between $3000 and $4000 a year at his job.

The outward appearance of the village has changed drastically since the war. At present in Kippel there are 71 private residential buildings, containing over twice as many complete units. Of these buildings, 32 were built before 1900, 15 between 1900 and 1945, and 24 since the war. With just under 100 households residing in Kippel, there is a large housing surplus, which can only be explained by the increasing tourist traffic leading people to speculate on new buildings; once the foundation and the roof are paid for, an extra story adds relatively little to the overall cost. A brochure distributed by the Lötschental tourist bureau advertises 31 different units in Kippel available to tourists who wish to stay in a private home, offering a total of 159 beds. At a rate of from five to eight Swiss francs per person per day ($1.16 to $1.86 in 1970), depending upon the season and the individual, the maximum income for the village could run as high as $300 per day for every day that the village is fully occupied. Considering the fact that in the peak summer season, and now more and more in the winter as well, it is frequently difficult to find lodging in the village, it would appear that the speculation is paying off. Of course, the same is true for hotels and consumer-oriented businesses in Kippel and throughout the Lötschental. The Gasthaus Kippel, recently torn down, was rebuilt with a capacity of 26 beds. The Pension Bietschhorn and Hotel Lötschberg (the latter only open in the summer) operate at near capacity during the peak seasons.

Provisions for tourists have altered other aspects of the village. A large communal field has been turned into a campsite, with room for well over a dozen tents. The road to this field from the village has been widened to facilitate traffic. Moreover, on the edge of the village a large parking area has been created to handle the growing number of vehicles. Some less apparent changes have also occurred. Older agricultural buildings are frequently abandoned, and if they are not converted into garages they are not maintained at all. Occasionally such a building collapses, in which case it is cut up for firewood and hauled away. An interesting feature of houses is the increasing prestige accompanying stone buildings. Until recently the church was the only large stone building in the village, due to the expense of building with stone on a relatively primitive technological level. Since wood has been the common building material used for centuries, it is only natural that stone should become a status symbol as it became feasible to substitute it for wood.

Much of the building on the perimeter of the village has been made possible by projects designed to minimize the danger of avalanche. Protective walls have been built and barriers erected to prevent the snow from breaking away high up on the alp, while forest growth has been increased in strategic spots to hold the snow. Other public projects include a road from Kippel to Hockenalp, a water system for private use and for fire hydrants, and a bridge across the Lonza below the village. Future plans include a road from Kippel to Kastlerwald on the shady side across from the village, the construction of a tunnel in a dangerous avalanche channel to the west of the village, increased street lighting, yet another school-house for an additional secondary school, a new sports plaza, and the extension of the chair lift up to Hockenalp.

One of the most serious problems created by the introduction of tourism as an important factor in the village economy has been the inflation of land values. Since the land is divided into small parcels, prices are considerably higher than if the units were larger, simply because there is no quantity discount in small sales and it is easier to demand and obtain a higher price when the total amount is relatively small. The injection of money into the economy by the developers has not helped the situation any, nor has the way they have spent it. The land they have purchased is situated just below the alp, and has always been poor quality agricultural grazing land. The prices paid by the developers for this relatively worthless land (as far as the villagers were concerned) have led the local people to demand much higher prices for land in and near the village, which they consider to be much more valuable. At the same time, the village has been undergoing an internal expansion, so that the inflation has hit the local residents the hardest since they can least afford it. If a man wants to build a house today he may have to purchase part or all of half a dozen parcels of land, which could cost him as much as 200 Swiss francs per square meter, or about $200,000 an acre based on current exchange rates. Of course no one in the village can afford much land at this price, but the cost of even a little bit of land can be enough to discourage a potential builder, or else put him deep into debt.

Continuing improvement in the transportation network within Kippel and the Lötschental has been of major importance in bringing about many of the changes described above. Without bus service to Steg, men would not be able to commute to the factory. The train carries many younger men north to Kandersteg and Frutigen and south to Brig and Visp where they are able to learn and practice their trades. The road network on both slopes above the village enables men to continue their agricultural operations to some degree without the heavy reliance upon communal labor which supported the village economy for so long. And finally the transportation industry itself provides jobs for a number of villagers, as workers on the railroad line, as bus drivers, mechanics, in taxi and chauffeur services, and in private hauling.

Expansion and improvement of the main lines of transportation into the Lötschental continue. The road from Gampel is being widened, with numerous tunnels planned in an attempt to keep it open for year-round use. The paved road has been extended from Blatten to Fafleralp, and is being widened up to Blatten, which promises to create new tourist opportunities at the rear of the valley. No longer will mules be used to carry tourists' baggage beyond Blatten. Other forms of transportation are also either being planned or seriously contemplated, primarily with an eye to tourism. The extension of a chair lift to Hockenalp in the commune of Kippel and the development company's plans for a cable car service from Wiler to their sites below Lauchernalp are examples of the branching off of transportation perpendicular to the main direction of the valley. Within the commune of Kippel several new projects are underway. The road to Hockenalp is being broadened and eventually will be paved to facilitate wheeled traffic up from the village. The road through the center of the village is being extended down to the Lonza, where a new bridge has been built, and eventually will be continued up into the forest on the shady side, where there is now just a dirt road.

While there has been a definite increase in the use of and reliance upon modern means of transportation among the residents of Kippel and the Lötschental in general, this cannot be seen as a primary motivating force in the rapid development of the transportation system. Certainly tourism must be considered in any discussion of transportation. In Kippel there are 16 personal automobiles (one for every 29 residents), two jeeps, five post office buses, eight motorbikes and 15 agricultural vehicles. The expense of the construction and maintenance of the network of roads, particularly those branching off the main valley road, is hardly justified by such a paltry number of vehicles, certainly not if these side roads are considered in terms of their contribution to the overall economy at this time.

STANDARD OF LIVING

Recent construction of newer, more modern housing in Kippel is a prime indication of the rise in the standard of living which has accompanied the modernization of the past decade. It is interesting also to compare the total income of the village just within the short period of 1960–1966, for which these figures are available. In the following table, the income is divided according to economic category. Despite an overall increase in the total income of almost 100% in this short period, agriculture declined in absolute figures by a third, in relative terms by two-thirds, from 9.1 percent to 3.0 percent. Major gains were scored in industry and tourism, as well as public services, illustrating the shift in emphasis from the primary to the secondary and tertiary economic sectors. (Note that the decline in construction income despite the building boom can be attributed to the increasing use of professional outside construction companies in place of local workers.) The same source also points out that few agriculturalists manage to attain the average personal income for the village. In 1966, of the 29 agricultural operations, 28 had an income of less than 3000 francs ($700), and the lone exception was listed between 3000 and 5000 francs (source: Statistik über die Fiskaleinkommen . . . 1966). Of course this does not include the

INCOME IN KIPPEL ACCORDING TO ECONOMIC CATEGORIES, 1960 AND 1966

Economic category	Income in 1960 (In Swiss Francs)	% of total	Income in 1966 (In Swiss Francs)	% of total
1. Agriculture	70,890	9.1	46,280	3.0
2. Tradesmen	120,112	15.4	249,130	16.0
3. Industry	23,204	2.9	225,675	14.5
4. Construction	152,741	19.5	89,895	5.8
5. Commerce & Trade	27,780	3.5	41,325	2.6
6. Transportation	63,603	8.1	51,880	3.3
7. Tourism	35,720	4.6	107,385	6.8
8. Professionals	37,115	4.7	110,050	7.0
9. Banking & Insurance	–	–	26,450	1.7
10. Public Services (gov't)	119,376	15.2	380,325	24.4
11. Subsidies	65,080	8.3	141,185	9.1
12. Miscellaneous	4,585	0.6	8,100	0.5
13. Property Income (rental)	62,532	8.0	78,740	5.1
Totals	782,738		1,556,420	

Exchange rate in 1970, 1 U.S. dollar equal to approximately 4.3 Swiss francs.

Source: *Statistik über die Fiskaleinkommen nach Wirtschaftsgruppen in den Jahren 1965–66.* Finanzdepartment, Sion.

agricultural yield which goes to support the household, but in any event a working capital of 3000 francs is hardly enough to keep an operation alive, let alone allow for personal cash expenditures.

An important consideration in the budgets of many Kippel residents is the additional income they receive in the form of government subsidies, totalling 9.1 percent of the entire income of the village in 1966, and certainly even more than that today. The federal government pays the equivalent of social security to every male over sixty-five and every female over sixty-two, the amount depending upon the earnings of the individual prior to retirement and his present material wealth; in 1970 the combined sum of old age (social security) and disability payments to various members of the village totalled approximately $55,000 per year. Other similar sources of income include widow's pension, child allowances from the factories and public service employers, and retirement pensions from the railroad, cantonal or federal government, and the Papal Guard. Of the 99 households in Kippel in 1970, 77 received some sort of outside aid. Most is in the form of child allowances or old age pensions, and the amounts are sometimes rather small, but the overall importance of this source of income to the financial state of the village must be emphasized. Particularly with regard to the maintenance of agriculture, which as we have seen is primarily in the hands of elderly men, pensions and social security are the crucial factors in the survival of a number of households.

The total amount of government subsidies to residents of Kippel for purely agricultural activities (excluding old age benefits) is on the whole extremely low, and plays a relatively small role in maintaining the agricultural economy. We might well ask, then, why any agricultural activity exists at all. The answer seems to be that the village agriculture has become either a hobby for the old men or a matter of convenience for a dwindling number of worker–peasant households. Milk and dairy products, vegetables and potatoes have been retained, but grains have largely been given up. Agriculture has ceased to pay its way in the village, and has become simply another contribution to the overall family income, in contrast to the prewar days when it supported the entire population of the village and was intensely practiced for want of a better livelihood. Today as the worker-peasant becomes more worker and less peasant he finds that agriculture is no longer compatible with the standard of living he is rapidly attaining, nor is it any longer a question of convenience—it becomes increasingly difficult to justify.

Perhaps the one significant factor in the minimal retention of agriculture, and an interesting exception to the rising standard of living, is the diet. Milk has remained important, as we might expect, despite the decline in the number of cattle kept by villagers. What has changed is the method of distribution and acquisition of milk and dairy products. The dairy cooperative in Kippel has long since closed down for lack of enough milk to render it profitable, but there is still a cheesemaker operating in Wiler and a centrifuge for homogenizing milk in Ferden. A few villagers take their milk daily to one or the other, but most of those who still have milk cows do not, preferring to sell it in the village. One man rationalized that his cows gave enough milk to feed his family, and by selling the rest he paid for all the cheese and butter his family purchased. This was much more sensible than making cheese and butter out of his own milk.

The shortage of cattle has made milk a marketable commodity within the village, and has in turn led to the almost total disappearance of domestic cheese. The chair lift and road up to Hockenalp enables girls on the alp to bring down a supply of milk daily in the summer, and in the winter the cattle are kept in stalls in the village. Here they receive more for the milk than it would be worth in any other form, including cheese. Last year the proprietor of the inn on Hockenalp actually had to purchase packaged milk brought in from outside the valley because there was a shortage of milk on the alp—all the cattle owners there had already made daily contracts for the sale of their milk in the village.

The decline in animals has also led to the replacement of household slaughters' by purchases from the local butcher in Wiler or from outside the valley. High prices of beef have turned many families to pork and mutton, far less expensive and usually more readily available. The recent introduction of deep freezers into the valley has enabled a change in the form of meat, although there is still a high preference for dried beef and dried mutton, no longer out of necessity but as a matter of taste. Freezers have also changed the purchasing pattern of meat, so that now many families buy a whole animal and slaughter it, rather than sharing in someone else's home slaughter and then reciprocating later on. However, despite the innovation in meat preservation, its consumption remains surprisingly low, in many households still only on Sundays and holidays. This reflects the conservative nature of the diet in the Lötschental even today, as indicated by the response of one young man when I inquired about the daily consumption of meat: "Who could eat meat every day? I'd get tired of it!"

po la to sta ple

po la

Although grain has all but disappeared from the domestic agricultural scene, bread is still a basic staple in the diet. White bread has replaced rye bread as the common commodity, the latter now relegated to the status of "Sunday bread," and made somewhat sweeter for the occasion. Potatoes are the other main source of calories, despite the insufficiency of the local crop. According to one informant, however, potatoes are no longer as important to the overall diet as they used to be, since so many other things can be bought today that were not previously available. Among vegetables cabbage is perhaps the most common, along with garden crops such as lettuce, beets, and leeks. Fruits are imported, with the recent exception of strawberries, and the trend has been toward co-operative purchasing in bulk from growers in the Rhone Valley. Itinerant merchants travel to the valley regularly when the weather permits, and in the winter supplies can be ordered by phone and delivered by rail and post bus. Itinerant merchants are also responsible for much of the local trade in clothing, bringing in dresses, pants, shirts, shoes, and work outfits, as well as other household wares. Catalog shopping is another common form of consumer trade in the Lötschental.

The normal diet of the Lötschentaler today reflects little change since the prewar days. The home economics class in the village school, which all girls are required to attend for two years, includes a major section on cooking, along with sewing, child care, home industry, and health care. Every school girl keeps a notebook of everything she cooks and learns about food during the two years. My observations over the year led me to conclude that the ideals of the home economics training in cooking were never reached in the home situation within the village. There are several reasons for this gap: the recipes the girls learn at school include some of the basic dishes common to all households in the village, along with several more intricate, though inexpensive, items. Nothing learned in class is beyond the means of the local residents—its purpose is to offer a practical education in every way. However, it can be stated without reservation that in matters involving diet, the Lötschental is boundless in its conservatism. Cooking techniques might be learned in school, but they are practiced at home, under the tutelage of older women set in their traditional ways, who inhibit any deviation from the time-tested patterns.

Conservatism is most evident, however, in matters of taste, where an extreme degree of ethnocentrism obtains. This is certainly not a situation limited to the Lötschental; we need only recall the history of the introduction of the potato in northern Europe to show that ethnocentrism and conservatism are characteristic of all societies where culinary matters are concerned. Rural, isolated peoples rarely exhibit cosmopolitan tastes. Exotic spices, unfamiliar foods, even new methods of preparation are generally summarily rejected. In many cases I found that even locally available items were not used, and frequently were misunderstood, not only by the older women in the village, but by the younger personnel in the school as well. Even a neutral attitude toward unknown dishes was rare. But what was most surprising, foods and methods of preparation common to other areas of Switzerland, known and understood by local residents and available to them, were still not used. Dietary conservatism can be brought out here as being the largest and most obvious gap created by the recent economic changes, as illustrated by the following conversation:

Anthropologist: What is your favorite Sunday meal?

Woman: We boil a piece of mutton in water, then take it out and drink the soup it makes. Afterwards, we eat the meat, but the soup is really the best part.

Anthropologist: Do you add anything else to this?

Woman: In the summer, when we have fresh vegetables, we put them in, too. But then it doesn't taste as good. It's better in the winter when it just tastes from meat.

Anthropologist: Well, then, why do you put the vegetables in at all?

Woman: Because it's healthy.

One of the most beneficial changes since the war, indicative of the rise in the standard of living, has been in the area of health care. The decline in the infant mortality rate, due in large measure to the presence of a doctor in the valley and the increasing reliance upon hospitals and modern medicine, has already been noted. In the prewar days the philosophy of self-sufficiency included not only the agricultural sphere, but extended to medicine as well. The isolation of the valley required its residents to rely upon home remedies and local medical care, and although a few such remedies are still used today, for the most part people rely upon professional medical care, either the doctor in Kippel or one of two physicians in nearby Gampel. However, a local healer in Ferden is still quite popular for broken bones and muscle and joint ailments. The many stories told of his successes tend to bear out the faith which local people have in his abilities. One young man claimed that were it not for this healer, he would not have been able to finish his apprenticeship training. He went to him with what was diagnosed as a broken ankle, and after just a few applications of salve and massages he was able to walk on it. He was certain that had he gone to a doctor for an X-ray, he would have been in bed with a cast on his leg for months.

Despite the tradition of giving birth in the home and the longstanding presence of trained midwives in the valley, most women today prefer to have their babies in the hospital. Older people are less willing to leave home when sick, and many look upon a hospital as a place where people go to die. Nonetheless the increasing frequency of the use of hospitals has been a strong factor in the decline of what were formerly major causes of death, such as appendicitis and pneumonia.

Many folk ideas about illness persist among the people of Kippel, even down to the younger generation. A warm southerly wind in winter brings on numerous complaints of heart trouble: "The *Föhn* (the name of this wind) causes a heavy pressure on my heart." Others complain of insomnia according to a particular phase of the moon. This is not to say that their analysis of their own conditions is inaccurate, but rather that the ascription of causation to particular meteorological phenomena borders on superstition.

One of the major health problems in Kippel today is dental care. According to the older villagers, before the introduction of white bread into the diet there was little trouble with tooth decay, and in fact the Lötschental was reputed to have had the best dental record in an official government study around the time of the first world war. The change in diet has not been accompanied by a change in dental hygiene practices, however, with the result that it is indeed rare for anyone over thirty to have a full set of teeth. The situation has deteriorated to the point where many young people simply have all their teeth out as a matter of course, to avoid prolonging what is to their mind a certainty. Government programs designed to increase the practice of brushing the teeth among school children, offering free examinations by a dentist periodically, have had little effect in Kippel. A quarterly session with a dentist is not enough to prevent the loss of teeth without cooperation at home from parents and children. Indeed, the situation is serious enough to have prompted one observer to comment that "cultural decay and tooth decay go hand in hand." (Müller 1969:135)

MARRIAGE

The pattern of marriage commonly found in Kippel has changed significantly in the last ten years. One of the first things a villager mentions when asked about change in the village is the fact that people marry younger today than formerly. In part this opinion is based upon an actual decline in age, but in part it is also based upon the perception that young people today are economically independent, which enables them to marry at a younger age whether or not they actually choose to do so. In fact, the age has fallen, from over twenty-nine years before the war to twenty-six in the sixties for women, and from over thirty-two to about twenty-seven for men in the same period.

Prewar marriages were commonly postponed due to economic considerations— the family had to have a sound footing before it began to grow. As one older man put it, a woman's "worry year" was not until thirty; today it is closer to twenty-five. Marriage was postponed also as a function of residence practices, and these too have changed over the years. Formerly a couple might wait until they had paid off debts accumulated by their respective families before they married, which might entail working outside the valley for several years. Another factor was the strong feeling that a man should have a regular source of income, and if the man were a farmer this meant he would have to wait until he came into his share of the inheritance. Since today most young men earn cash incomes, settle in new houses and not with their parents, and have no back debts to pay off, none of these impediments to an early marriage is very important.

The newly married couple of half a century ago usually lived with the parents of either the bride or the groom, and did not move into their own home until they began to have children and were' crowded out. Today this is no longer the case. The newlyweds seek to set up a separate household immediately, and in this regard the building boom which Kippel has witnessed in the postwar years has been of major importance to the residence pattern. Undoubtedly many young couples would have moved out of the village, probably to the town where the young man earned his living, were it not for the housing surplus in Kippel. As it is, several have left despite the opportunity to find inexpensive, comfortable housing in their native village.

With women marrying younger today than a generation ago we might expect to find larger families, but exactly the opposite is the case. Whereas in the first quarter of the century the average number of children was 6.6, this figure declined to 5.7 for the second quarter, and in marriages between 1950 and 1959 it has fallen to 4.6. (Obviously the figure cannot be computed for the 1960s, since young couples are not through having children.) Several factors seem to account for this trend: while women are marrying younger, they are not having children for as long; the average spread from first to last child has dropped from 10.8 years between 1925–1949 to 8.1 years between 1950–1959. Also important has been the changing attitude toward family planning. Today many women in the village are able to admit that too large a family is not always a good thing, without feeling they are contradicting the teachings of the church. The main point of contention is how to limit the size of the family, but there is general agreement that it is a good idea. Reduced family size can probably be at least partially attributed to a greater awareness and understanding of the church-approved rhythm method, coupled with an increasing use of more modern and efficient methods of birth control among the younger girls.

SUMMARY: SOCIAL CHANGE, 1960–1970.

As we have seen, since the war Kippel has turned toward the outside for its economic needs. New jobs, new sources of income, and ideas for consumption have penetrated the isolation of the Lötschental primarily through contact of an economic nature. The introverted prewar village has given way to the extroverted postwar village. A clear result of this change in focus of attention has been an overall decline in participation in village affairs by those who have found work or developed other interests outside the valley. In many cases this has led to an outright discontinuation of traditional activities, but even more important it has weakened many bonds which formerly held the village together so closely. Owing in part to an emulation of high prestige urban trends, in part also out of deference to convenience, the social life of the village has taken on a new dimension for the older residents, while the attitudes of the youth are almost from the very beginning foreign to those of their elders.

Until ten years ago practically everyone stayed in the village, certainly at least through adolescence. Today of the young men in the village only a handful work there, and only one has had no extensive direct contact with the outside, either through work or apprenticeship. For the older villagers, having already grown up in a certain kind of environment, which we could call traditional, they are now being subjected to a set of values, goals, and ideals which are in conflict with their background. For the youth, on the other hand, both systems—the traditional and the modern—are being thrust simultaneously upon each person who has contact with the outside. The problems of integrating two systems into one pattern of behavior are different for them, and their options and solutions are consequently not always in line with those of their parents. A generation gap has developed, based upon entry into the continuum of change at different points in time.

Attempts have been made with increasing frequency to forestall this process of social change, while at the same time maintaining and even increasing the rate of economic change. That such attempts are being consciously made is perhaps an indication of the alarming alacrity of the social change affecting Kippel. On the local level, a common theme in the sermons delivered in church and at public affairs by the village clergymen is the maintenance of custom within the village. Recalling the days when Kippel was the most important village in the valley, they claim that through social conservatism it can remain so, whereas if it attempts to match the wealthy cities in their cosmopolitan character it is doomed to failure. Of course, there is a note of anxiety attached to these sermons, fearful as they are of the new "liberal morality" found in the metropolis, but they invariably include direct suggestions toward the maintenance of tradition.

Perhaps because of the open contradiction of economic progress with social conservatism, many of the youth fail to understand the forces operating in the village today. One young man, for example, told me that eventually he wanted to settle elsewhere, for he found the village "primitive." Upon further questioning, he admitted that he felt the village setting was "backward" and the life "boring." When he said he thought the houses were backward, he did not mean the comfort or the facilities available within the village, but the style of construction and the general appearance of the cluster of buildings in the village. Another slightly older man expressed his feelings when he observed that the festivals had lost their old aura of frivolity and gaiety, and had taken on instead a sort of sadness. The people, he claimed, drink too much and carry on as if forced to do so. He concluded that this was all due to the rapid state of change causing the disappearance of customs, old traditions, and old values in general. The meaning of such festivals, and of social interaction overall, was different from what it is today.

An interesting development in the village recently points to a new attitude toward the not-so-distant past taken by many villagers. In the summer of 1970 a village museum was opened, exhibiting many items of the material culture from the prewar agricultural days. The museum was initiated and sponsored by the late Albert Nyfeler, an artist who came to the Lötschental early in the century and settled permanently in Kippel. While it is true that he was an outsider, with a different perspective of his village, still the project as a whole has met with generally favorable reactions from the natives of Kippel, several of whom cooperated in compiling and setting up the initial exhibition. The realization of the need for preserving the past implies an awareness that change has occurred, and that more is imminent.

The federal government has taken an active interest in preserving the past in the remote mountain valleys throughout Switzerland. Under a law which provides for the preservation of national historical sites, the community was denied permission to replace the old wood-shingled roof on the church tower with a new copper one. In some cases, local village governments have gone even further, with ordinances prescribing not only the materials but the architectural styles of new buildings and the repairs and maintenance on existing ones.

The makeup of the population of Kippel has changed very little over the years. Over 99 percent of the residents are still Roman Catholic, and all are native German speakers. Ninety-two percent of the population are citizens of Kippel, and a remarkable 91.6 percent were born there. Clearly the homogeneity that was always such a marked feature of Kippel is still prominent. The population has increased rapidly since the war, 35.9 percent between 1941 and 1970. While we cannot say with certainty that occupational change was the prime force enabling such an increase, it is highly probable that without another source of income the valley's agricultural resources could not have supported as many people as now reside there. The system of land use, and particularly fragmentation and its maintenance through the inheritance practices, are extremely vulnerable to population pressures, and are likely to break down under continued growth unless another outlet is found. On the one hand a new source of income allowed for an increased standard of living without straining the agro-pastoral economy of the valley any further. One the other hand, however, increased emigration has plagued the Lötschental since the war.

The figures on emigration cited earlier show that more people have left Kippel since 1950 than in the entire first half of the century. Before the war the most frequent emigrants were those who went off with the army or who joined the Papal Guard. Emigration in the era of the agro-pastoral economy was severely restricted by poverty, both the local poverty of the valley and that of Valais and the surrounding area in general. The fact that there was little industry and for all practical purposes no prospect for regular employment outside the Lötschental served to keep people from emigrating, while a similar force was exerted by the local system of inheritance and land distribution which gave each villager the opportunity to survive. As unappealing as the prospect of a life of poverty in the Lötschental must have been to so many people, it was always better than the prospect of starvation elsewhere. Even within the valley, the worse conditions became, the more the people relied upon their traditional system of cooperation and self-sufficiency. The psychological dependence upon the home community, continually reinforced by the social system which stressed communal action in overcoming hardship, was enough to keep most villagers at home.

Since the war new opportunities have opened up to men and women from the Lötschental in Valais and in many large cities and towns throughout Switzerland. The hotel industry has created an increasing demand for the labor of young girls, and although when not working they tend to return to their home village, they are put in contact with men from other areas of Switzerland, so that their matrimonial opportunities are significantly increased. Many girls have emigrated from Kippel since the war, and although personal histories are not available for all of them, it can be assumed that the vast majority who married outsiders did not meet them in the Lötschental.

For the men, emigration has been a means of escaping agriculture and finding more modern and better paying employment. The opportunities for industrial employment in Kippel are minimal—aside from the knitting factory and a few odd jobs around the village, men must commute to the factory in Steg or to other Valaisan towns. The same is true of training for the younger boys, most of whom are in apprentice programs in Brig, Visp, or Steg. They are willing to commute to and from work daily as long as they have no wife and family, but most express the opinion that the long train and bus ride each day would take up too much time if they were married. As it is, many boys in Kippel leave on the 5:00 A.M. bus and don't return until 7:30 P.M.

While they are in a training program most boys live with their parents in Kippel and commute daily or weekly. This is frequently the only possibility, for they earn very little as apprentices, certainly not enough to live on. Once they begin to earn a full wage they tend to spend more time in the town where they work, and many even take rooms there to cut down on commuting. Although it is still too early in this stage of occupational change to tell what the trend will be, most of these young men feel that they will eventually settle outside Kippel. A few express this attitude with great reluctance, but the majority seem to prefer life in the town to the quiet isolation of the Lötschental.

The people of the Lötschental perceive emigration as the major problem confronting the valley today. They blame it on a lack of industry, the poor state of the present tourist industry compared to other valleys in Valais, and the general lack of opportunity for employment and advancement here. In 1970 alone at least two households (12 residents) left Kippel for the Rhone Valley because of the problems of commuting. One man, whose work took him out of the valley daily, was forced to move because his health would not allow him to drive up to the Lötschental from below every day. Another man, trained as a chef and formerly employed in the tourist industry in Kippel, gave it up in favor of a job with a major industrial concern in the nearby town of Visp. These two cases are invariably cited by local residents who complain about the lack of opportunity in Kippel and in the Lötschental in general. They strive for more education and specialized training, and then when they get it they find they cannot use it here, so they emigrate. The only ones left in Kippel are those who have not learned a trade, and who have not gone on with their education, and this in turn widens the gap between the isolated Lötschental and the wider society.

An important effect of emigration is that it has modified the natural age spread in Kippel, so that the young and old are relatively more numerous than previously. We can see this by comparing the age pyramids for the village from 1941 and 1970.

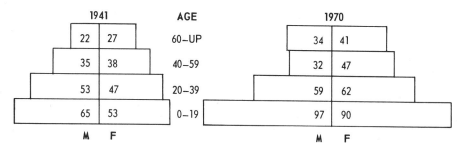

1941		AGE	1970	
22	27	60–UP	34	41
35	38	40–59	32	47
53	47	20–39	59	62
65	53	0–19	97	90
M	F		M	F

Of course, improved health care and reduced infant mortality have contributed to this shift, making the overall trend very clear. Since 1941 the proportion of the population under twenty has risen from 34.7 percent to 40.5 percent. Similarly, the relative number of old people has increased from 14.4 percent in 1941 to 16.2 percent in 1970. To counter these rises, the proportion of villagers between twenty and forty has dropped from 29.4 percent to 26.2 percent, and those between forty and sixty have declined from 21.5 percent to 17.1 percent.

As noted earlier, the basis for stratification within the village had already been replaced when cash incomes became common in the 1950s. Tourism has contributed to this change to some extent in the 1960s by placing large amounts of money in the hands of a few villagers. Those who have been able to build large houses or set their sons up in business have certainly benefited in terms of rising prestige in the community. But status within the village is based on more than simply increased income. A dual set of standards has evolved in the ranking system in Kippel, which separates economic from social prestige. This is perhaps necessary because many of the young men who have become economically successful outside the valley have done so at the expense of their ties with their fellow villagers. A young man may earn a lot of money, build a new house and support his family comfortably, for which he earns a certain amount of prestige. But this is not the same type of recognition as a man who participates in civic affairs will receive. The nature of work outside the valley often prohibits one from participation in communal activities, but since community service and allegiance to one's family are equally important values, each is rewarded independently.

It is necessary to mention economic mobility, for it is an important feature in the overall determination of the levels of social ranking. Yet, as we have seen, it frequently works at cross purposes by raising an individual's prestige through increased income, yet lowering his actual position in the community by removing him from the day-to-day activities that are so important to the villagers. A few are able to combine the benefits; they work outside but devote themselves completely to their village. Many more are literally prevented from doing so by the nature of their employment. The extent to which occupational mobility is actually limited within the Lötschental can be documented by observing the younger generation in Kippel today. Of 60 men employed between the ages of eighteen and thirty-five years of age, only 13 found full-time employment in Kippel, or for that matter anywhere in the Lötschental. They include two who work full time in agriculture, four in transportation, three in local consumer outlets, a barber, an electrician, a plumber's assistant, and a teacher. The Kippel job market is saturated, with few possible openings in the near future. Since no significant industry exists in Kippel, and since the possibility of education or continued training beyond secondary school is nonexistent, few positions are open for professional workers or people trained in technical skills. On the contrary, only outside the valley can the newly trained apprentices practice what they have learned. Fifty male residents of Kippel have received special occupational training of some sort, however slight. Yet of these 50, only nine have been able to use their training in work in Kippel, and of those, four are bus drivers. Clearly the ties holding a man to his village are much stronger if he is able to have continuous contact with his fellow villagers, particularly through his occupation. This, then, is the focus of the problem of emigration.

An interesting example illustrates how the younger people feel about mobility. In one family in the village all the grown children except one have acquired further training; two daughters have become nurses, one son is a mechanic and another a draftsman. A third daughter declined the opportunity to continue her education, saying she wanted to be home more often, and if she learned a specialized skill or trade it would keep her away; but her case is exceptional.

The movement of the focus away from the village has led to a change in the form of interpersonal relations, with effects extending to the makeup and participation in voluntary associations within the community. New associations have grown up with the occupational groups, so that today in Kippel there is an association of metal workers (actually including all men from the valley who work in the aluminum factory in Steg), a group formed by the railroad workers, and another for construction workers. These are loose associations of men with little active occupational interest off the job, and they serve only a minor function in the village life. On the other hand, sports clubs and youth groups seem to be thriving in Kippel today, for they offer their members geographic mobility as well as recreation. Soccer tournaments are organized, championship ski races are held in every village and again for the entire valley, and in general competition is keen and participation is high. Some of the more traditional associations have declined in popularity recently, and in one case, the theatrical club, lack of interest led to its dissolution. However, most associations have met the challenge of the modern economy and have emerged successfully. The village band, which started out on a budget of less than a hundred francs, recently purchased new instruments and uniforms at a cost of about 70,000 francs. The group raised the money itself through soliciting donations and by holding special events such as lotto games, sponsoring dances, and giving concerts.

Relations of friendship and comradeship among villagers are also different today now that so many of the men are away from the village so much of the time. Factions or even strongly identifiable cliques have not arisen around occupational interests, but according to many informants the character and intensity of personal contact, particularly among men, is no longer the same as it used to be. Conversations are more fleeting and the sharing of experience is less compelling among men who do not share the same livelihood. When all were agriculturalists in an isolated valley, they all had the same interests, but today the scope of the Kippel economy has broadened and the spectra of interests of various individuals no longer match each other.

Finally, the nature of contact within the family has changed to some degree due to the absence of the father from the village. Men no longer exert the control over their children, particularly their sons, that they once had, for the children come in greater proportion under the protective care of their mother. The father's leadership is lacking, and his impersonalized work, in which the rest of the family cannot take part, lessens his authority with his children (Niederer 1956:52).

One of the most noteworthy aspects of stability among all the change that Kippel has experienced in recent years is the high degree of participation in religious rituals, exemplified by the attendance rate at Sunday church services. While it is not unusual in European rural peasant communities for women to participate actively in the local religious practices, the men frequently take a rather passive role. In Kippel, however, men attend services regularly almost without exception, and they speak freely in public of having fulfilled their "Sunday duty." Indeed, the old use of the term "Sunday" to refer to a day of obligatory church attendance has been retained and is commonly used to refer to any such holy day, even though the factory worker must still report to work on his regular shift and must therefore think of "Wednesday-Sunday" or "Friday-Sunday." The woman who runs the local bakery once explained to me why it would be such a busy week for her: "Tomorrow is Thursday and I have to bake a special batch of Sunday bread (a rye bread baked only for Sundays and holidays) because the next day is Sunday. Then comes Saturday and I have to bake another batch for Sunday, but it has to be a double batch, because Monday is Sunday too!"

What is so remarkable about the religious attitudes of the people of Kippel is that they have been maintained in the face of a general decline in the importance of the church in the secular life of the village. With the integration into the wider society and the consequent increase in participation in secular events and a secular ideology not directed toward the church and the village, there has been more dispersion within the daily life of areas which were formerly controlled by the church. At the same time, church rules have grown less strict and forceful, in part a result of the changes emanating from Rome itself. Many villagers, old and young alike, express confusion and displeasure with the rash of new rules and changes in ritual practices which have filtered down to them in recent years. Some continue earlier practices in spite of the new rulings, while others claim to have taken matters into their own hands with the notion that if they follow their own conscience that is all that is required of them.

The young people in the village are every bit as religious as their parents, but in the wake of changes they have witnessed, both secular and temporal, many have begun to reinterpret some of the teachings of the church on a personal basis. This is not to say that they are the first generation ever to do so, but rather that the pressure for absolute conformity within and through the church is no longer as strong as it used to be—the priest no longer rules with an iron hand. Older residents recall the austerity of the old days, particularly the holidays which required fasting, and compare it to practices today. Formerly fasting was taken very seriously by churchgoers in Kippel, so much so that a total fast was prescribed from dawn till dark. Today, of course, the church no longer requires fasting on most Fridays, and on many other holidays, and even when it is required most villagers limit only the intake of certain kinds of food, primarily meat. As one informant described the situation, "People have less fear of God nowadays."

Perhaps the most indicative example of the changing attitude of youth toward certain aspects of the religious practices of their church occurred when a soccer tournament fell on the same day as Church Dedication Day, a major religious holiday in Kippel. A local team was entered in the tournament, and on the team were several young men who normally participated in such ceremonies, either in the band or as soldiers in the honor guard parade. The team competed nonetheless, for as one member explained, it was only a six-man team and they would hardly be missed in the ceremony. Besides, it was an important tournament.

Not unexpectedly, a decline in the traditional forms of recreation has paralleled that in some of the traditional religious ceremonies. Religious festivals as well as secular celebrations have taken on a new appearance, and modern media have intruded upon the old forms of entertainment. Villagers agree that the major religious holidays are nothing today in comparison to previous years. Old traditions not associated with any particular holiday, but indicative of the old way of life in the village, are also dying out. The traditional feminine dress, called the *Frauentracht*, is worn less often today. In recent years women have stopped wearing the *Tracht* except on major church holidays and special occasions, much to the dismay of the local clergymen, who long to see a return to the old Lötschental traditions. Other means of expression and art forms, such as the carving of inscriptions on new buildings, or behind-glass painting, which is unique to the Lötschental in all of Switzerland, have likewise disappeared. Only mask carving, with its popular appeal to tourism, has expanded.

New forms of entertainment have been introduced to the Lötschental. Old patterns of interaction, such as reciprocal visits in private homes or even traditional courting patterns, have been replaced by public gatherings. Concerts, dances, and public parties are very popular today. Money raising functions are also well attended, particularly lotto games or competitive card games sponsored by a local organization. And just within the last year, the introduction of television into the valley and its immediate adoption by the various taverns in the village promises to cut into the traditional card playing activities of the older men as their interest shifts to the new medium.

Sports have become the most important preoccupation of the young villagers, particularly with the introduction of popular magazines and now television, promoting local and national heroes. Soccer is popular among boys in the summer, and skiing arouses interest not only through local competition, but on an international level as well. Until recently only boys could ski, for most families could not afford skis for the girls as well. A few girls who tended cattle on the upper slopes during the winter learned to ski, but not so much for the sport of it as for its utilitarian value in getting to and from the stalls. Moreover, until a few years ago girls never wore slacks, a distinct handicap to any skier. Today ski races are among the most important social events in the Lötschental. A championship race held in Kippel in 1970 attracted 124 contestants from all four villages in the valley and from other places as far away as Basel. Some of the better local skiers also venture to other valleys to compete in races.

A final word on social change is called for with regard to education and its importance in the events of the last quarter century. Prior to the war children attended primary school in Kippel for six months each year. They were usually finished at age fourteen or fifteen, and went right to work in their parents' agricultural operation. Today in Kippel there is a primary school, a secondary school,

Contestant in the Lötschental ski championship.

a home economics class, and a private preparatory school (*Progymnasium*). One hundred and thirty-six students attend school in Kippel, divided into six classes. Seventy-three attend primary school, in three grades covering a total of seven school years. Another 25 are in secondary school for a term of two years, while 25 attend the parochial prep school and 13 girls are in the household class. Students are required by law to finish nine years of obligatory schooling, including seven years of primary school and at least two years in some other form, which could include household school, secondary school, or under certain circumstances an apprentice program which includes classroom work.

Surprisingly few students are able to qualify for secondary school after finishing their seven year primary education. An entrance examination must be passed before the student is accepted, and apparently most youngsters are unable to matriculate. Despite the fact that they are given a second chance a year later, after repeating a year of primary school, the enrollment in secondary school remains low—the 25 students represent all four villages of the Lötschental. Boys who do not qualify usually end up in trade school, while girls go on to household school. Apparently the major reason for the lack of emphasis on higher education is a perceived limitation on mobility within the wider society. Trade schools offer careers in areas where a generation ago no Kippel resident could expect employment, and the aspirations of parents in Kippel today rarely extend beyond this limit. Only two young men from Kippel are presently studying beyond the secondary school level. Far more typical is the example of a boy who finished secondary school and enrolled as an apprentice mechanic at a nearby factory, only to have his father pull him out at the last moment because he needed help in remodeling his house.

Many parents, having had little education themselves, yet emerging from the recent economic change relatively successful in terms of the local scene, look upon "too much" schooling with suspicion. They consider it impractical, and fail to recognize the opportunity for mobility outside the valley because of their lack of familiarity with urban ways. Perhaps they also fear the loss of their children through emigration, a sort of low-level "brain drain," although this sentiment has never been openly expressed by any parent for fear it would be interpreted as selfishness.

It is difficult for a foreigner to assess the quality of education the students in Kippel schools receive. The subject matter is frequently different from that in U.S. schools, and the teachers are trained differently. The low rate of advancement into secondary school, however, suggests an inadequate preparation in the fundamentals of learning, and it is quite probable that lack of parental concern or at least parental assistance contributes to the problem. The major dilemma in education today is that teachers are not always adequately prepared themselves. If local people are able to get enough education, they frequently do not return to the valley. Yet the villagers prefer to have less qualified natives teaching their children rather than better qualified outsiders, and in light of their attitudes toward outsiders the reason for this is clear. Despite lengthening the school term to nine months and introducing a more varied curriculum, the educational opportunities in Kippel are simply inadequate to meet the demands of the wider society.

7 / The future

All told, the rate of social change in Kippel has not kept pace with the economic transformation the village has experienced since the war. Nor is this an unexpected sequence under the circumstances. The social isolation of the Lötschental lasted well into the 1960s even though economic links with the outside preceded those of a social nature by more than a decade. When we consider that not until the mid-50s was the paved road extended beyond Kippel, it is not surprising that many of the attitudes and practices of the older people do not conform to the standards of the more cosmopolitan urban and semiurban society of the Rhone Valley, where most men today earn their living. What the future holds for Kippel, and how this gap will be bridged, will be discussed in this final chapter.

WORLD VIEW

A number of changes in attitude have been alluded to in the previous discussion of Kippel over the last generation, as former peasants gradually became integrated into the industrial economy and the village grew less isolated in time and space. Indeed, the observer can take the position that the world view of the average Kippler has changed considerably in the past twenty years, and cite numerous examples to prove it, as I have done up to now. But I would not be presenting the whole story if I did not stop to mention the equally significant ways in which the outlook of the typical villager has failed to change. This "old-fashionedness" will become important in assessing the potential for change in Kippel in the 1970s.

The experiences and opportunities open to people from Kippel have helped to give them a broader perspective on their relationship to the world around them. Sports activities are but one of many ways in which Lötschentalers have been able to increase their contact with the outside world. Employment in the Rhone Valley and in the major cities of Switzerland draws off a significant portion of the local work force, and thereby enables young people to broaden their horizons. For the older folk in the villages, however, this is not the case. Almost without exception, they are limited in their experience to Upper Valais at most.

Despite the increased geographic mobility, traditional ideas of distance are still prominent, focusing at the same time upon a social distance as well as a physical separation. The big cities of Switzerland, even those where German is spoken, are looked upon with awe by many of the older villagers; tales of what goes on in the city are the basis of a complete misconception of what the urban scene is actually like. The younger generation is beginning to understand and break through this social barrier, particularly through occupations which allow them to work in the cities and commute to the Lötschental on weekends. But even so, problems can arise; one young man who works in a large city told me he could never marry a local girl and live where he works, for she would be forever homesick, despite the fact that it is only a few hours away by train.

Modern media are the most important factor in opening up communication between the outside world and the Lötschental. Unfortunately, they create only a one-way channel, and in order to participate in the culture which they present, the local resident must leave the valley. So far the media have led to contact only with Upper Valais for the most part, but it will be interesting to see what the effects of television will be upon the Lötschental. Not only are aspects of the overall Swiss culture introduced into the local scene for the first time through TV, but foreign cultures are presented too, though often in a way in which they could never hope to be understood. During my last month in Kippel television was finally introduced, and the prime-time fare included American programs dubbed in German. I found it literally impossible to explain the point of the program "Julia," which deals with a currently unmarried, middle-class black nurse and her young son. Detective shows were also popular—but how can a valley without a policeman comprehend the typical television portrayal of crime in an American city?

The telephone has become more important in recent years in the Lötschental, so much so that a new centralized operation has been set up just east of Kippel to handle the increased demand for service in the valley. Many homes already have telephones, which are looked upon not only as a status symbol, but as a functional addition to the local scene. Every villager has access to a telephone, either through the post office or the public phone booth on the street in the middle of the village. As more young people have taken jobs outside the valley yet maintained their residence in their native village, the telephone has taken on increased importance in maintaining the ties of kinship and friendship. It is also becoming increasingly important for the growing consumer interests in the valley which demand more immediate contact with the outside.

On the other hand, increased contact with the outside world through travel and modern communications media has failed to alter many of the deeply ingrained beliefs and guiding principles of the people of Kippel. The attitude toward dental hygiene is symptomatic of a more widespread world view, a fatalistic attitude in which little value is placed upon preparation, preventive measures, and regularity in social obligations. Foresight has so often been negated by the harsh climate with its frequent catastrophes that the local population has become hardened to the futility of planning. The result is that even on the level of personal inter-action, plans are rarely carried out; *ad hoc* events are much preferred, and the placing of a date and time on an event is often seen as an intrusion upon people's lives. This avoidance of prearranged activities perhaps accounts for the lackadaisical attitude of many villagers toward the proposed tourist development in Wiler. They have very little faith in the ultimate success of the development, and find it difficult to comprehend the overall effect it will have on their lives. It is almost as if they don't believe what is happening to them, and after it has happened they don't believe it will happen again.

Such an attitude seems to account for the apparent lack of business sense found among some local consumer-oriented merchants. In one store the supply of beer ran out the day before Christmas, the peak of the winter tourist season. The reported reason was an oversight by the proprietor, and his refusal to stock a larger inventory when the tourist trade would logically call for more of everything, particularly something as important as beer.

The general attitude of local residents toward outsiders has apparently changed little in the last century, for there is still a great deal of hostility toward tourists today. The villagers don't seem to mind as much when the same people come back again and again, and even build or buy summer homes within the village, but they resent the large-scale, impersonal appearance of hotels and apartment buildings that keep the tourists from ever having contact with the local culture. Their attitude is often reflected in their treatment of individual tourists. It is difficult to generalize on such a subject without going into ramifications of personality differences, but I witnessed countless cases of local residents abusing tourists (and indeed at least as many the other way around), either by showing their resentment when required to serve them, or by attempting to take advantage of them. One man, describing a sale he had just made to the development company, said "They are like that junk yard on the road to Brig. You can sell them anything." This attitude is reflected in many dealings with foreign tourists.

Other aspects of the world view of Kipplers have changed in recent years. The prudishness fostered by the church so strongly in past decades is less evident among the young people of today. They interact more freely and are more relaxed about it than in the days when the priest forbade all unsupervised contact between the sexes. The older people look upon this as a natural result of increased contact with the outside world and the introduction of a money economy which has liberated the youth of today, but that is not to say that all of them necessarily approve. Indeed, many resent the independence of today's youth.

Another change in the ethos of the villagers has been the decline of the jack-of-all-trades, which seems to have accompanied the removal of the worker from direct contact with the finished product of his labor. The agriculturalist had to do everything for himself, for he could not afford to hire a specialist. He made his tools, doctored his animals, and built his own house. Today's villager is inundated with the notion of the specialist and the Germanic penchant for titles, to the point where he frequently feels inadequate to do the same kinds of things that he did twenty years ago. Even a job as simple as painting a door calls for someone trained as a painter.

Certain new ideas have been accepted by the conservative mountain peasants only with great difficulty. One such example is women's suffrage. In 1970 the men of Valais went to the polls to vote on extending suffrage to women. (Women still did not have the right to vote nationally, and in the true spirit of the Swiss confederacy, it had to come from the cantons first.) Most of the men in Kippel doubted the value of allowing women to participate in formal decision making, but they were reluctant to vote against it. The real reason, it subsequently came out, was not that the man feared domination by their wives. As one male informant put it, "If a man can't control his wife and convince her how to vote, then he shouldn't be married."

Rather, the passage of the women's suffrage act in Kippel was a face-saving act by the men. Through various media they had become aware of the "progressive" nature of the movement for women's rights, and among themselves had become convinced that eventually women would acquire the right to vote in Valais and in Switzerland. Aware of their image as a backward and highly conservative valley, the men from Kippel (and from the other three villages in the Lötschental) voted overwhelmingly in favor of the bill, and were rewarded for their "modernity" when their vote was reported, as is the practice for every election, on the front page of the major newspapers in Valais. This example is perhaps the best illustration of culture lag in Kippel, for it shows how men who know what the modern world expects of them can act in a way they consider "proper," without ever understanding the modern basis for their actions and without ever sacrificing or changing their outmoded traditions.

It is at times like this that the attitudes of some of the older villagers provide an element of humor, since they seem to be so improbable in today's modern world. An amusing incident in Kippel points out the extent to which property is personalized, particularly among the older people who recall the days when it was all they had. In the process of widening the road leading from the village down to the Lonza, it was necessary to tear down two old agricultural buildings. One was removed without incident, but when it came time to raze the second, the owner complained. An old woman owned half of the barn, and she refused to sell out to the village, claiming that she had no need for money and she wanted her barn. As it was explained to me, the village council could have acquired the barn anyway through eminent domain, but it would have required a court hearing and they were in a hurry to finish the road before winter set in. What finally happened was that two councilmen measured the barn and determined what portion of it was hers, and then literally cut off the rest of it with a saw. This gave them room to widen the road.

THE ECONOMY IN THE 1970s

We have seen how a rise in the standard of living has accompanied increased income through occupational diversification since the war. Certainly this is a very strong plus for the valley, for no matter what the nativistic Swiss might think about their peasant heritage, no matter how much they might wish to preserve a mountain peasantry today, the prewar era of poverty with its malnutrition, debt, and overall suppression of the ambition and mobility of the mountain folk is a grisly chapter in the history of the Lötschental. For the

Lötschental there is no future in the past. The future lies with the youth, who though proud of their mountain stock, nonetheless are a part of the era of progress. They are not interested in reviving an old-fashioned economic system that can only handicap them in the modern world, nor do they want to return to an antiquated social system that sets them up for ridicule in the very society in which they seek their fortune. As a result, many of them make a clean break with their homes and set out to start anew.

Emigration is the most serious problem confronting the Lötschental today, and the prospects of it subsiding are not good. In order to keep young people in the valley, there must be training programs in which they can learn the skills necessary to compete on today's job market, and then there must be work for them in which they can apply these skills. So far only a handful of local residents have found satisfactory employment in their home village. The tourist industry will provide some incentive to stay on, for it will contribute to a more cosmopolitan, more exciting atmosphere in the valley by introducing a style of social life that is more in line with the wishes of today's youth. It is doubtful, however, that the jobs to be found in the proposed tourist development will be adequate for the needed transformation of the economic focus of the valley, for as will be shown, the development is proceeding with little consideration for the natives of the valley.

One solution to the dilemma of employment is to utilize the excellent transportation facilities to bring in unfinished products which can then provide jobs for local people in small local factories. Late in the summer of 1970 one such operation was in the preparatory stage; a watch factory was to be set up in a private home in Kippel, which would employ several young people from the village. This is an excellent example of the possibility of injecting outside capital and resources into the economy in order to curtail emigration. Other such programs could be developed, perhaps with government assistance, and they would certainly meet with more success and at less cost than the present government policy of wasteful subsidies to unproductive mountain agriculture.

Economic problems of a more general nature must be solved if the valley is to move ahead at a faster pace. At the moment the most pressing problem is the insistence of the Swiss government upon maintaining agricultural operations in the mountains without altering the basic structure of mountain economic institutions to conform to the demands of modern society. If the government feels that mountain agriculture and indeed mountain residence is necessary for the national defense (which is itself a moot point), then it must be willing to step in and adjust such barriers to rational economic activity as land fragmentation, inflation of land prices, lack of mechanization (what little is possible near the valley floor), and partible inheritance. The government cannot argue that it fears the effects upon the cities of a major population movement within Switzerland from the mountain valleys to the industrial centers, for it is presently experiencing difficulties with a foreign labor force imported from the Mediterranean countries due to a shortage of native workers. The argument, rather, seems to be to keep the mountains productive, and this could be accomplished as easily by large-scale rational agricultural concerns as by individual peasant holdings.

In the profit-oriented postwar economy, it is cruel to promote the type of minimal mountain operation found in the Lötschental when it only serves to hold back the population from greater economic gains in other fields.

But rational agriculture depends primarily upon land consolidation, and that is something which cannot be carried out without outside pressure. An example of the futility of mechanization without consolidation is seen in the case of a farmer who recently acquired a gathering machine, a sweeperlike vehicle that picks up the hay as it drives over it, depositing it in an attached trailer. Although the machine is obviously designed for a situation whereby speed is more important than 100 percent efficiency, in this case it was supplemented by a trailing crew of women who raked up what was left behind and carried it to the barn. Moreover, it was used on fields so small that it could not turn around, but had to be driven back and forth in the same direction.

Maintaining agriculture in the Lötschental without at the same time contributing to emigration requires not only consolidation of the land and subsequent subsidies for machinery, but it must be preceded by the introduction of a new philosophy of work. As long as the worker–peasant cannot find spare-time income more remunerative than a small-scale agricultural operation, he will not give up his farming, and thus large-scale farming by others will be hindered. Higher wages will help in the sense that the younger generation will become more attuned to the consumer-oriented, time-oriented media and less willing to continue their predecessors' self-sufficiency complex. But ultimately, spare-time activities must be found for the people. Mask carving is one possibility, with the prospect of a growing market as the influx of tourists continues to increase. Other possibilities, perhaps even wage labor on large-scale farms during peak periods, must be developed in order to convince the worker–peasant to give up his holding.

What specific measures can be carried out in Kippel? Some immediate changes could be instituted as stopgap measures to stem further fragmentation, while long-range plans can be made for an overall amelioration of the patterns of ownership and inheritance with regard to rational economic activity. For one thing, while there are countless cases of the division of parcels in the village cadastre, there are none of consolidation, the reason being that there is no mechanism for consolidating land in the land register. Parcels are charted on maps and given numbers, and while they can be subdivided (by giving the number an "a" and "b" section), they cannot be combined. In other words, if a man acquires two adjacent pieces of land from two different sources, although he works them as one unit they are treated as separate for inheritance purposes. In Wiler recently the area purchased by the development company was consolidated on the village records. Such a task in Kippel could not be accomplished completely until maps were made to cover all the land lying within the communal boundaries, and new procedures were instituted to facilitate the recording of consolidation. Subsequently, the cantonal law admitting partible inheritance would have to be reversed to prevent consolidated parcels from being divided again with each new generation.

Perhaps consolidation will not be completely effective until government policies begin to change. At present subsidies for various agro-pastoral products provide incentives to the small-scale operator. The psychological difficulties inherent in consolidation can be overcome if the government removes the incentives from the worker–peasant, and replaces them with strong incentives to the large-scale farmer.

It is difficult to say just how many large-scale agricultural operations using modern methods and machinery can be supported by the land available in Kippel. Former agricultural statistics and animal counts can give us some indication, but a good deal depends upon the types of machinery available and the overhead of such an operation. Nonetheless, it is certainly reasonable to expect that several farmers operating on a profit-oriented basis could earn a good living in Kippel, while providing as much if not more for their fellow villagers than under the present system. In fact, one evening I engaged in a long conversation with a young man from Kippel who has reluctantly found work outside the valley. He said he would gladly return and work the land, if only there were a way of making a living at it, but that it would be impossible on the present scale of operation found in the village. Certainly he is not the only one who feels this way.

TOURISM IN THE 1970s

A major shift in economic activity within Kippel must be accompanied by the creation of new opportunities for local residents. While it might appear that agricultural operations there today are highly irrational, requiring an inordinate amount of time and labor for such a small yield, nonetheless when measured in terms of the opportunity cost, their persistence is self-evident. That is to say, the net effect of agriculture for the worker–peasant in Kippel is a gain rather than a loss in terms of his opportunity to add to his income in other ways. He views his agricultural operation in terms of his total spectrum of possibilities, and as yet he has no better alternative. The shift from small-scale worker–peasant operations to large-scale, profit-oriented farms in Kippel is above all predicated upon the introduction of new opportunities for those who do not go into farming.

The future of tourism is of course pivotal to the future of the Lötschental, but it is difficult to be optimistic about its effects upon the local population. Although Swiss law prohibits any foreigner from owning land without special permission, an exception was made for the investment company now developing a resort area above Wiler. It is difficult to see the logic in bringing in foreign capital at the expense of the local community where it is to be spent, although governments are frequently inclined to think in terms of statistics and reports rather than human beings. Certainly the valley will benefit by any additional income, particularly in light of the failure of the Swiss government to propose any realistic solution to the emigration problem. Then, too, the existing tourist industry already owned and operated by natives will be able to expand and flourish under future conditions as projected by the development company. But this is merely a drop in the bucket compared to the potential earnings of the foreign investors, and if the valley is really to thrive on tourism while at the same time maintaining its self-respect, it would be preferable to have local control over the development and a greater share of the profits on levels other than that of the lowest salaried laborers.

The sad fact appears to be that the residents of the valley are inadequately prepared for sophisticated economic planning, even on a level much less important than the multi-million dollar investment proposed for Wiler. A few individuals might be capable of comprehending the needs of such a program and organizing the project, but the lack of leadership in the Lötschental prevents a concerted effort from attaining success. Previous attempts have failed dismally. A few examples of my own experiences might better illustrate the obstacles to a broad development of tourism, at least in Kippel. The mayor of the village, supposedly the political leader of the community, displayed open hostility to my presence in the village and my proposed research. This sort of defensive attitude toward outsiders is not uncommon among villagers, and is manifested in various forms of hostility to new ideas and new approaches to old problems. The less cooperative the village leaders are with outsiders, the less able they are to formulate plans for future development along the lines of their own perception of the needs and goals of the valley.

In another example, a self-styled young organizer from the village once asked me to translate a letter into English, so that he could send it to a foreigner who had advertised money to invest. I did this for him, and later was shown the reply and asked to explain it. When I told him that the man charged a commission for finding investment capital, the villager became very indignant that someone else should make a profit on what he considered to be his own ideas. This lack of financial sophistication emerges as a major handicap to locally controlled development. Minor undertakings in the past have not been successful, and today the village of Kippel finds itself in debt. Most of the indebtedness is due to public works projects financed in part by the village, but significantly enough the chair lift in Kippel is a major source of the village's financial distress. Originally a tow bar built by a local resident (with financial backing from an outsider), it had to be taken over by the village when the owner could not keep up the mortgage payments. The village decided to convert it to a chair lift so that it could be used in summer for travel to the alp, at a cost of over $100,000. Today because of high maintenance costs, limited use, and continued high interest rates, the chair lift costs the villagers approximately $10,000 annually, in addition to the mortgage payments.

Aside from the apparent inability to comprehend the financial complexities of the modern world which are so important to the initial stages of a major tourist development, a fundamental lack of understanding of the services required by tourism is in evidence. This is not only my own opinion, but the view of a prominent villager. "People around here are too intolerant of tourists," he said. "If someone comes into a restaurant five minutes late for a meal, they scowl at him. They don't understand that people will pay for extra service—they have the money, and they demand the service. The English (in Wiler) know that, and they will succeed because they treat people differently. Until we understand that in Kippel, it will be difficult to promote tourism on our own account."

The resolution of the problem of tourism in the Lötschental does not appear imminent. On the one hand, the lack of sophisticated and effective local leadership is a handicap to internal growth. On the other hand, the outsiders who appear to be well on their way to reaching their goal of a major resort development still display an extreme ethnocentric bias, deriding local customs and practices, resentful of the intrusion of local residents into "their" resort. Perhaps this would be the case no matter what, but one gets the feeling that if the proper care had been taken to supervise local internal growth, many of the most flagrant abuses of the local population could have been avoided. What the final result will be, and what its effects upon the population will be, it is too early to say. One cannot in good conscience advocate the denial of a higher standard of living to a population that has suffered from a lack of economic opportunity for so long, yet one must warn of the consequences when a population is forced to alter its basic life style in so short a period of time. The major institutions and patterns of interaction, the goals and ambitions of the people, all will be changed, possibly only in return for the scorn of a temporarily transplanted group of strangers.

The nativist looks upon the alpine peasant society as something which should be preserved at all cost. Tourists express their displeasure upon seeing machinery replace the hand tools of the traditional agriculturalist. They long for the ideal mountain peasant, the *Bergbauer*, and they long to see the traditional mountain life, with the happy peasant, hearty and healthy, hard at work in his traditional economic system. "The good old days," "the salt of the earth," "the foundation of our true democracy"—they want to preserve a living museum in the isolated mountain valleys of their country.

Theirs is a dream that can no longer be. Communications have cut down the barrier between country and city. The final intrusion, television, will eventually assimilate the mountain peasant into the life style of the city. It is only a matter of time. What is to be hoped for at present is enough protection for the mountain people that tourism, or any other form of economic advancement thrust upon them, can be mollified to the point where they can adapt their way of life to their new socioeconomic environment, rather than having it molded for them. The example of the industrialization of Valais suggests that this has been the case so far. Examples of tourist development elsewhere, coupled with the conditions under which tourism is being advanced in the Lötschental, suggest that it might not be the case much longer. Writing about communal labor, Niederer said: "Perhaps the purity of this piece of ancient village life could be maintained, but it is senseless to want to retain an empty form" (1956:90). It is just as senseless, I think, to destroy it in the name of progress, when it could be allowed to die a natural death on its own.

References

Anneler, Hedwig and Karl Anneler, 1917, *Lötschen.* Bern: Academische Buchhandlung von Max Dreschel.

Bachmann-Voegelin, Fritz, 1970, *Die traditionelle Kulturlandschaft einer Berggemeinde (Blatten im Lötschental).* Zürich: MS.

Beerli, André, 1961, *Unbekannte Schweiz: Wallis.* Translated from the French by Irmgard Vogelsanger de Roche. Touring-Club der Schweiz.

Bellwald, A., 1963, *Raumpolitische Gesichtspunkte der industriellen Standortwahl in der Schweiz, erläutert an den Möglichkeiten einer Industrialisierung der Oberwalliser Bergdörfer.* Zürich: Polygraphischer Verlag.

Berthoud, Gérald, 1967, *Changements Économiques et Sociaux de la Montagne.* Bern: Francke Verlag.

Bloetzer, Hans (ed.), 1964, *Lötschen und sein Prior.* Winterthur: Verlaganstalt Buchdruckerei Konkordia.

Cole, John W., 1969, Economic alternatives in the Upper Nonsberg. *Anthropological Quarterly* 42:3:186–213.

Dumont, R., 1966, *Types of Rural Economy.* (Translated from the French, first edition 1954) London: Methuen.

Hallenbarter, Antoinette, 1946, *Berufs- und Verdienstmöglichkeiten der Jugend des Lötschentales, Jahrgänge 1920–1930.* Diplomarbeit der Schweizerischen Socialcaritativen Frauenschule, Luzern.

Imboden, Adrian, 1956, *Die Produktions- und Lebensverhältnisse der Walliser Hochgebirgsgemeinde Embd und Möglichkeiten zur Verbesserung der gegenwärtigen Lage.* Brugg: Verlag der Schweizerischen Arbeitsgemeinschaft der Bergbauern.

Kämpfen, Werner, 1942, *Ein Burgerrechtsstreit im Wallis, rechtlich und geschichtlich betrachtet, mit einem Überblick über das Walliser Geteilschafts-, Burgerschafts- und Gemeindewesen.* Zürich: Berner Dissertation.

Kaufmann, Beat, 1965, *Die Entwicklung des Wallis vom Agrar- zum Industriekanton.* Zürich: Polygraphischer Verlag.

Kurtz, John W., and Heinz Politzer, 1958, *German: A Comprehensive Course for College Students.* New York: W. W. Norton.

Leibundgut, Hans, 1938, *Wald- und Wirtschaftsstudien im Lötschental.* Dissertation ETH Zürich. Bern: Buchdruckerei Büchler.

Loup, Jean, 1965, *Pasteurs et Agriculteurs Valaisans: Contribution à l'étude des Problèmes Montagnards.* Grenoble: Imprimerie Allier.

Müller, Carl, 1969, *Volksmedizinisch-geburtshilfliche Aufzeichnungen aus dem Lötschental.* Bern: Hans Huber.

Niederer, Arnold, 1956, *Gemeinwerk im Wallis.* Schriften der Schweizerischen Gesellschaft für Volkskunde, Band 37. Basel: Buchdruckerei G. Krebs.

———, 1969, Überlieferung im Wandel: zur Wirksamkeit älterer Grundverhaltensmuster bei der Industrialisierung eines Berggebietes. *Alpes Orientales* V:289–294. Slovenska Akademija Znanosti in Umetnosti.

Schmid, Carl, 1969, *Bellwald: Sach- und Sprachwandel seit 1900.* Basel: Buchdruckerei G. Krebs.

Siegen, Rev. Prior Johann, 1959, *Der König des Lötschentals.* Illustrated by Albert Nyfeler. Bern: Paul Haupt.

————, 1960, *The Lötschental: A Guide for Tourists.* Translated by Ida M. Whitworth. London: Titus Wilson, Kendal

————, 1965, Kippel—Vergangenheit und Gegenwart. In: *75 Jahre Musikgesellschaft Alpenrose.* Publication in honor of the 75th anniversary of the Alpenrose Music Society, Kippel.

Statistik über die Fiskaleinkommen, 1966, Cantonal Statistics on Annual Income by Class of Occupation According to Commune. Sion.

Stebler, F. G., 1907, *Am Lötschberg: Land und Volk von Lötschen.* Zürich: Albert Müllers Verlag.

Unstead, J. F., 1932, The Lötschental: A Regional Study. *The Geographic Journal* 79:4:298–318.

Weiss, Richard, 1941, *Das Alpwesen Graubündens. Wirtschaft, Sachkultur, Recht, Alplerarbeit und Alplerleben.* Erlenbach-Zürich.

Wolf, Eric, 1966, *Peasants.* Englewood Cliffs, N. J.: Prentice-Hall.